Coming to Term

Albert.
Great to be working with
you ... All the best to
you and your
beautiful family!

Bill

Coming to Term

A Father's Story of
Birth, Loss, and Survival

William H. Woodwell, Jr.

University Press of Mississippi
Jackson

www.upress.state.ms.us

The author has changed some of the names of real
individuals appearing in the narrative to protect
their privacy.

Library of Congress Cataloging-in-Publication Data
Woodwell, William H.
Coming to term : a father's story of birth, loss, and
survival / William H. Woodwell, Jr.
p.   cm.
ISBN 1-57806-374-4 (cloth : alk. paper)
1. Woodwell, William H.   2. Infants (Premature)—
Biography.   3. Fathers—Biography.   4. Father and
infant—Biography.   I. Title.
RJ250.W66   2001
362.1′9892011′092—dc21
[B]   00-054574

British Library Cataloging-in-Publication Data available

Lyrics from "The Story of Life" by Jimi Hendrix are
reprinted by permission of the board of directors of
Experience Hendrix, L.L.C.

For my family

Prologue

When I first set out to write the story of the extremely premature birth of our twin daughters, Josie and Nina, I thought of the experience as a kind of therapy, a way to explore my feelings about what was happening, a way to vent. I also thought that my account of the events surrounding our girls' birth at twenty-four weeks gestation—each weighing less than a pound and a half—would be a valuable document to have down the road, something our family would treasure as we reflected back on a period when we were reminded every day of the fragility and the preciousness of life.

As time went on, however, I came to feel that this story had meaning beyond our family. I was so affected and so moved by what had happened to us—the experience had forced me to think anew about so many of my assumptions, so many things I felt I had already figured out—that I imagined it might somehow affect others in a similar way. I imagined it might encourage people to cherish their own lives and their own children just a little bit more.

Just the same, I have always felt more than a little guilty about turning the events of the summer of 1997—events I will never forget—into so many written words. When I finally decided to try to make this a story for a wider audience, I couldn't shake the feeling that I was taking advantage of the situation in a way, using my family's horrible experience to jump-start a long-dreamt-of career as a writer of books.

But the truth—or at least I hope it's the truth—is that putting this story together has had very little to do with my dreams of a bucolic life as a writer, apart from convincing me once and for all that writing is a hard, hard thing to do.

So what was driving me, really? What was making me set aside days and entire weeks to piece together this narrative, to learn more than I ever wanted or needed to know about modern medicine and the workings of the human body, to revise the manuscript again and again until I felt it was as good as it would ever be, until I felt it was a legitimate recounting of the events surrounding our daughters' birth and of what Kim and I were feeling and thinking as those events unfolded?

The answer is that I am dying to tell this incredible story to whomever I can—not only because I think there are lessons in these pages about life and how we live it, but also because I am proud. Proud of my daughters for convincing me once and for all to treasure life. Proud of my wife for enduring untold insults with an honest and a gritty grace and for always putting the babies' interests first. Proud of our marriage for coming out stronger despite the enormous stress of the experience. And proud of the family, friends and neighbors who were there for us and our daughters in our time of need.

Searching the Internet over the last several months, I have found dozens of stories about children born too early who beat the odds and survived. So eager are the parents of these children to tell the stories of their babies' tortuous first weeks and months that they have set up special web pages with names like "Believe in Katie Lynn," "Oliver's Story," and "Saving Grace." The stories often are told in excruciating detail. Images of babies tiny and sick in their hospital warming beds are transposed with pictures of the same children, at two or three years of age, smiling like nothing happened and playing with a ball or a pet at home.

Before our daughters were born, I might have thought that these other parents had lost it, that they were too wrapped up in their children and the circumstances surrounding their birth. I might have thought that they should put the whole experience behind them and get on with their lives. But now I see that these parents are exceedingly normal. Now I understand completely why they feel so compelled to tell the world about their children and the trials they faced.

George McGovern, writing about his daughter Terry's life-and-death struggle with alcoholism, observed the following: "I was open about Terry's death not only because it was virtually impossible to be silent about it, but because I wanted both her life and her death to be understood and appreciated—and I wanted others to gain from the lessons her life can teach us."

Just as Terry's story was much more than a story about alcoholism, this is much more than a story about pregnancy or premature birth. Rather, it is a story about life—about how it surprises us, how it is so often beyond our control, how it can hang by the thinnest of threads, and how, in the end, it is something to be cherished and loved. And it is also a story about what we can learn from even the smallest human beings—the little ones who enter the world weighing less than a large drink at the 7-Eleven, their lives on the line from the day they are born.

Coming to Term

One

Kim's visit to her doctor on the morning of May 27, 1997 was supposed to be no big deal, just a regular checkup to see how everything was going. At the time, Kim was twenty-four weeks pregnant with twin girls. She had just started on a schedule of seeing the doctor every three weeks, with ultrasound appointments scheduled for every six.

I was working in my home office that morning when Kim called from the doctor's. "They're sending me to the hospital," she said matter of factly. She said her blood pressure was high and that she had protein in her urine, two signs of something called preeclampsia. Kim said it probably meant she'd have to spend the summer on bed rest. She said they'd have to do more tests. When I asked how she was feeling, Kim said she was fine.

"I feel perfectly fine," she said. "I don't understand it. I feel fine."

I told Kim I'd meet her at the hospital as soon as I could, and I rounded up our three dogs to bring them inside. I then set out on the thirty-five-minute drive north to Winchester, Virginia, the nearest city to the Shenandoah Valley farmhouse Kim and I had moved to from Washington, D.C., just two years before.

The idea of Kim in bed all summer long was disturbing; I wondered how she could possibly stand it. But if that was the price we had to pay, then so be it. We already expected Kim would be on bed rest in the final month or two because of the twins, or at least on "limited activity," as Kim's doctor had called it. This was happening a lot sooner than we expected—we were sixteen weeks shy of the girls' mid-September due date—but I figured we would somehow deal with it. We would somehow cope.

I met Kim in the recovery room on the hospital's labor and delivery floor. She was alone, dressed in a hospital gown, and lying atop the sheets in one of the four or five beds lined up like parked cars against the wall opposite the recovery room door.

Kim was in an OK mood, it seemed, forcing a smile now and then, but obviously perplexed at how this could happen when things seemed to be going so well. Throughout the preceding five months, she had been extremely conscientious about her health. She walked every day, avoided alcohol and caffeine, and followed all the basic diet guidelines in the pregnancy books without getting fanatical about it.

Besides, high blood pressure had never been a problem for Kim before. Why was it a problem now? She had been a healthy person all her life, and I imagined her wondering if she was in a dream, wondering if she wasn't really in a hospital bed but in her own bed at home, still pregnant without a problem but with her subconscious making a show of the inevitable anxieties lodged deep in an expectant mother's mind.

I perched myself uncomfortably on the low, rolling stool beside her bed. Kim told me the nurses had taken a second urine sample, this one through a catheter. They also had taken blood for various tests to find out more. The results weren't back yet.

Kim then handed me a brochure that one of the nurses had given her on preeclampsia. She said she'd been too agitated to read it herself. She said she'd read it later.

Leafing through the piece while we waited for the test results, I learned that preeclampsia affects as many as one in ten pregnancies in the United States. The primary signs are high blood pressure, protein in the urine, and swelling, or edema. The most severe cases can lead to convulsions—eclampsia—and even death. Although bed rest and other measures can help prevent preeclampsia from advancing to a more critical stage, the only known "cure" for the condition is to end the pregnancy. Often, doctors will have to deliver the baby early to save the mother's life. As a result, preeclampsia accounts for an astounding one-third of all premature births.

The cause of preeclampsia, the brochure told me, is not known. More often than not, it affects woman who are pregnant for the first time and women who are either under twenty-five or over thirty-five years of age. Kim was thirty-three at the time; this was her first pregnancy. Other risk factors include chronic high blood pressure, kidney disease, and diabetes, none of which was a problem for Kim. One risk factor that might have been a problem, however, was the fact that Kim was carrying twins. I later found out that preeclampsia occurs in as many as three in ten twin pregnancies.

Kim and I waited in the recovery room for what seemed like hours. After two other women were admitted to the room, I pulled a curtain around Kim's bed for privacy. One of the other women was pregnant with twins, too. From her conversations with the doctors and nurses, I made out that she was farther along in her pregnancy than Kim, but it was still early. One of the twins, apparently, was much smaller than the other and they were going to have to deliver that afternoon. The woman disappeared as quickly as they brought her in.

I remember thinking that Kim and I were lucky. Our problem, it seemed at the time, was manageable. And our babies appeared to be doing all right.

But soon we got a sense that our problem had become less manageable than we thought. There suddenly seemed to be a lot of activity and a lot of talk in the nurses' station outside our room. Through the door, we could hear a male voice saying something about needing transportation—either an ambulance or a helicopter—and needing it fast. Kim told me the voice belonged to the doctor on call, the one who had seen her when she first arrived.

One of the nurses finally came in and told us the blood tests had turned up some "more concerning news." "More concerning than preeclampsia?" we asked. She nodded yes and said to sit tight until the doctor could come to explain. He was busy with a delivery, she told us. We figured it was the other woman with twins.

Within minutes, the nurses had Kim hooked up to an IV of magnesium sulfate. They told us this was standard procedure for preeclampsia, that it would help stabilize her blood pressure and keep her from going into seizures. The nurses also gave Kim a shot of steroids—betamethasone—into her behind. When we asked what the steroids were for, one of the nurses explained that they would help the babies' lungs develop if we had to deliver early.

I remember Kim's eyes when the nurse mentioned the possibility of early delivery. And I remember an unblinking look of fear and helplessness, like she'd been caught in the headlights of an oncoming truck. We were only twenty-four weeks along. Kim had just recently started to show. How early a delivery were they talking about?

We were alone in the recovery room for another ten minutes or so before one of the nurses came in to explain that Kim was going to have to be transferred to the University of Virginia Medical Center in Charlottesville that afternoon by ambulance. It would be a two-hour ride. When we asked why, the nurse explained that the Winchester hospital couldn't take care of babies born before twenty-eight weeks gestation.

The doctor was through with his delivery and returned to see us at about two o'clock. We had been sitting together in the recovery room since noon. He explained that they wanted Kim in Charlottesville as soon as possible, "in case you have to deliver the babies," he said. When we asked what the problem was, the doctor explained that it appeared to be a severe form of preeclampsia called HELLP syndrome. The doctor said they'd be able to do testing in Charlottesville to find out more. It was clear from his all-business demeanor that he wanted us out of there fast—uncomfortable, I'm sure, about the thought of having to deliver extremely premature twins himself.

Kim began to cry after the doctor left us alone. "I don't even believe this is happening. I feel fine. I'm doing fine." All I could do was hold her hand and say, "I know."

Soon one of the nurses was back with some paperwork we had to sign. She said she'd be going along for the ride in the ambulance with Kim. She asked if I wanted to follow in our car.

I said no. While we were waiting for the doctor, Kim and I had agreed that I would stop at home before leaving for Charlottesville so I could water the plants and take the dogs up the road to the woman who boards them when we're away. Then I'd pack some clothes for both of us—two or three days' worth, maybe. It was hard to think much farther ahead.

When the ambulance drivers finally arrived, they helped Kim shimmy from her recovery room bed onto a transport gurney, careful to move her IV equipment with her, along with the catheter that was now collecting Kim's urine in a plastic, see-through bag.

During the ride down in the elevator, the others were talking casually about the weather and work. At one point, the nurse told the ambulance drivers she was on until eleven o'clock that night and was "glad to get away for awhile."

Outside, I gave Kim a kiss on the forehead before they loaded her into the ambulance. "I'll see you in Charlottesville," I said. She barely responded, still stunned by the events of the last several hours. I could see she was trying hard to hold back more tears.

Two

The half-hour drive home from the hospital in Winchester was a blur. It appeared that Kim's pregnancy was nearing an early end, and I didn't know what to think. I remember turning the radio on and then off. I was picturing Kim lying flat on her back in the ambulance as it made the two-hour trip to Charlottesville. I wanted to try just to *focus,* to get a handle on what was happening to us. But I couldn't. There was too much uncertainty, too much we didn't know.

Back at the house, the telephone rang as I ran in the door. It was Kim's mother calling from her home in Boston just to check in, to see how things were going. My heart raced as I started to explain our day. Stumbling over my words, I asked her to let me catch my breath and I sat silent for a moment with the phone in my lap.

"We still don't know a whole lot," I finally said after putting the handset back to my face.

I told her we'd call from Charlottesville that night with more information, something Kim and I had planned to do already.

After hanging up the phone, I packed a couple of bags, watered Kim's plants, loaded the dogs in the car, and took off up the road to leave them with our neighbor. On the way out of town, I returned a movie we had rented the night before. I was a little embarrassed, I remember, thinking about video late fees at such a time. But I wasn't sure how long we'd be gone. Days? A week? After realizing I hadn't eaten since breakfast, I picked up a drive-through dinner at Wendy's by the interstate and was on my way. It was about six o'clock when I was finally on the road.

Now that I had spoken with Kim's mom, I figured I should probably use the car phone to call her dad; they were divorced and both in the Boston area. I reached Jim at home. He already knew. Apparently, Kim's mother had phoned Kim's sister, who quickly had phoned their dad. I told him I didn't have a lot of information. I said I'd call him later, too.

Jim told me to drive safely. He actually said it twice, probably imagining me careening down the interstate like something out of a Mad Max movie.

The only ones left to tell now were my parents, but I decided to wait. I knew they were due that night at an awards dinner my older brother had organized back home in Pittsburgh. And I figured they had already left the house. The idea of leaving a breathless and worried message on their answering machine struck me as stupid. What would I say?

Charlottesville is about an hour and forty minutes from our home in Shenandoah County—south on I-81 through the Shenandoah Valley and then east on I-64 over the Blue Ridge. I had made the trip a couple of times before to visit Monticello and the University of Virginia with visiting family and friends. It's a beautiful drive, with postcard views of farmland and mountains all the way, but it didn't even occur to me to enjoy the scenery that late spring evening. I might as well have been driving through a tunnel.

Along the way, I phoned two of my clients and left messages that I'd be out of touch for the next few days. And I turned the radio on and then off again, wanting but unable just to think.

At the hospital, I told the man at the front desk that my wife had been admitted to labor and delivery. He asked her name and then joked with a couple of elderly women he'd been talking to that I looked like a nervous father to be. They all laughed.

I took the elevator to the eighth floor, found Kim's room, knocked, and entered. She was lying in bed, with two IVs now pumping medications and fluids into her left arm. Several machines were stacked on the table beside the bed, their green, orange and red readouts painting a cryptic, moment-by-moment picture of how Kim and the babies were doing.

Kim already had a remarkable variety of devices and wires attached to her body. There were monitor leads, a blood pressure cuff that was set to inflate every fifteen minutes, and a red light clipped to her left index finger to record the oxygen content of her blood. She also had two round monitors—each about the size of a large peppermint patty—strapped to her belly with elastic belts to record the beating of the babies' hearts.

The room was surprisingly large, with a bathroom by the door and two big windows on the far wall looking out toward the mountains and over the emergency entrance where they had brought Kim in. The room temperature was cool to counter the effects of the magnesium sulfate, a drug that can make a patient feel uncomfortably hot. The only sound in the room was the clop-CLOP-clop-CLOP-clop-CLOP of our babies' heartbeats amplified through the fetal monitor machine. Kim said later they sounded like horses.

"How are you feeling?" I asked, putting down the bags I had brought from home and leaning over Kim's bed to kiss her.

"I was fine until I got to the hospital this morning," Kim said, trying to force a smile. "Now I'm just hot."

There was a knock at the door before Kim and I had a chance to talk. It was a young woman in green scrubs. She introduced herself as a medical student and explained that our babies would need surfactant when they were born. A soapy substance that a baby's lungs don't start producing enough of until about thirty-six weeks in utero, surfactant coats the lungs and helps them function so they don't collapse. At UVA, the medical student told us, they were working with a synthetic surfactant that they felt was better than the surfactant hospitals traditionally had used, a product extracted from cows. She asked if we'd be willing to participate in an ongoing trial of the synthetic stuff. We said sure and signed some papers.

"So we're really here to deliver the babies," I said to Kim after the medical student had left. It was half a question, half a statement of the facts as I understood them at the time.

Kim said it sounded that way. She told me the doctors had been in earlier to explain everything. She had asked them to come back when I arrived so they could give us both the full story. Kim wanted me to hear it too, not from her but from them. Medical information, we quickly discovered, loses an enormous amount of its factual basis in translation from one nonexpert to another. It's like a big game of telephone, with the doctors telling you one thing and, by the time it gets to a friend or family member, it's totally different.

The doctors were back in our room within minutes. There were three of them. Because UVA is a teaching hospital, it is rare that you talk to just one doctor about anything. Throughout our stay, we played host in our room to an ever-changing cast of residents, interns, medical students, and attending physicians, not to mention the nurses whose shifts were practically impossible to track. By the end of our time there, I imagined someone could come in off the street, take Kim's blood, give her an injection, and leave without us suspecting anything was wrong, as long as they were wearing scrubs and looked remotely like they knew what they were doing.

The doctors confirmed that Kim had HELLP syndrome and that the only cure for the condition was delivery of our babies. They said the plan was to wait until Kim's vital signs indicated she was getting sicker and then to do an emergency C-section.

"We want to give the babies as much time as possible inside their mother, but our primary goal is to save you," one of the doctors told Kim. Every day they were inside Kim would give the babies a 2 to 3 percent better chance of survival, the doctors said.

HELLP syndrome affects approximately 10 percent of pregnant women with preeclampsia or eclampsia. The incidence of the disease in the United States is about 1 per 150 live births. The maternal mortality rate is 3.5 percent, and as many as one in four babies born to women with HELLP do not survive, usually because of premature birth. The survival figures for these infants are misleading, however, because a HELLP baby's chances depend almost entirely on its gestational age when delivered. The earlier the disease presents itself in a pregnancy, the worse off these babies are.

Basically, HELLP happens when the liver becomes involved in preeclampsia; the most common cause of death in HELLP cases is liver rupture. The key features of the syndrome are what give HELLP its unfortunate name. They are: hemolysis, or the breaking down of red blood cells; elevated liver enzymes, a sign of liver malfunction; and low platelets. A cellular component of the blood along with the red and white blood cells, platelets promote clotting after an injury.

The doctors said that based on their experience, they expected it would be just a couple of days before Kim's condition became worse. They'd seen women go longer than that, but it was rare. The hope was that we could make it to Thursday noon—forty-eight hours after the initial dose of steroids—so they would have time to take effect and strengthen the babies' lungs for life in the outside world. The doctors told us they planned to give Kim her second steroid shot later that night. Normally they'd wait twenty-four hours between doses, they explained, but they wanted to put Kim on an accelerated schedule just in case.

After the doctors left, I sat on the edge of Kim's bed and we cried. It had all come to this. All the back-and-forth about whether to have children; all the thinking and talking about what we'd need; all the books, the articles, and the prenatal classes; all the morning sickness Kim had endured; and all the excitement about the twins. And now here we were, a hundred miles from home in a hospital room in Charlottesville, Virginia, sixteen weeks before term and waiting for Kim to get sick—very sick—so the doctors could cut her open and bring our babies into the world too early. Our twins.

"It's not even their fault," Kim said through her tears. "They were doing great."

"I know," I said. I suspected Kim was in some way blaming herself for what had happened, wondering if maybe it was something she did, something she ate. "It's nobody's fault," I said, trying to reassure her. "It's nobody's fault."

Before trying to get some sleep that night, we called our parents to bring them up to date on the day's events. The waiting had begun. We promised to keep everyone informed about how things were going and said we'd call again as soon as there was news.

Later, after Kim dozed off, I pulled our copy of the book *What to Expect When You're Expecting* from one of the bags I had brought from home. I had seen it on the way out the door and packed it in case we had questions. Looking up HELLP syndrome, I found only a short footnote in the section on high blood pressure during pregnancy—nothing we didn't know already. I then jumped to the section on what to expect in the sixth month of pregnancy, wondering what our babies looked like, where they were in their development and growth: "By the end of the sixth month, the fetus is about 13 inches long and weighs about 1³/₄ pounds. Its skin is thin and shiny, with no underlying fat; its finger and toe prints are visible. Eyelids begin to part, and the eyes open. With intensive care the fetus may survive now."

The word "may" had never sounded so foreboding, so negative, so loaded with doubt. Considering that we were only at the very beginning of the sixth month, I wondered if our babies even had a chance. I went to sleep that night to the clop-CLOP-clop-CLOP-clop-CLOP of our babies' heartbeats, wondering if they had any idea what in the world was going on. Wondering if they were ready to live.

Early Wednesday morning, I made the first entry in a journal of our experience that I would keep for several months. I started the journal on the laptop computer I had brought to Charlottesville from home. Those first few days in the hospital, I got in the habit of documenting our experience at times when Kim was sleeping. I would sit by the window in the red vinyl chair that converted awkwardly into my bed and type away, emptying my thoughts onto the screen.

Wednesday, May 28, 0600: Their hearts beat on like nothing's wrong. Kim says they sound like horses. Do they know something's different? That things have changed? I wish I could tip them off somehow, get in there and tell them they need to be ready. Give them a pep talk. It's hard enough coming into the world the way most of us do. For them, it will be that much more of a surprise, that much more of a shock. Fact is, we're essentially powerless to help them now, except to keep them in there as long

as we can. For every day they stay in their safe little world,
they've got a better chance of making it in ours.

Three

The news that Kim was pregnant with twins hit me like a brick. It had taken more than six years of marriage before we finally decided to have just one baby, and now we were having two. When Kim broke the news after an initial visit with her doctor—"So who in your family had twins?" she asked with a devilish smile—my thoughts quickly turned to the added responsibility and the added headaches that a second child might bring. I imagined simultaneous college tuitions, along with two of everything a child needs—from cribs and car seats to orthodontia, school clothes and, later, cars of their own.

Within minutes, maybe hours, however, I became genuinely excited about the whole thing. Twins! It was so unexpected, so different. It started to sound like a lot of fun.

Of course, the fact that there were two fertilized eggs growing inside Kim in the sixth week of her pregnancy was no guarantee that we would have twins. After the initial ultrasound, Kim's doctor explained to her that pregnancies often start out as twins but pretty soon turn into single births; one of the little ones just doesn't make it. Recent studies, in fact, suggest that as many as half of all pregnancies viewed by ultrasound before the eighth week show two gestational sacs in the uterus. In two-thirds of these cases, only one sac remains after the tenth week.

"If they're both still there at our next checkup, then it'll be more of a sure thing," Kim told me.

She showed me the sonogram printout. Sure enough, there they were: two little round blobs of white floating side by side, almost touching, against the black.

"Like little headlights," I said. "Coming at you."

My exposure to twins had been minimal. I had seen *The Shining* several times and was deathly afraid of meeting identical twin girls in the hallways of deserted mountain resort hotels. In addition to that, I had grown up spending summers on an island in northern Ontario with my mother's twin cousins, Hetsy and Lolly, and I went to boarding school in Connecticut with identical twin girls from France who insisted on rooming together the entire four years. Everyone thought they were kind of strange.

And Kim, it turns out, had a grandmother who was a twin. This might have explained everything—apparently, twin genes pass along more reliably on the mother's side—but our doctor later told us she was pretty sure ours were identical twins. The membrane between them appeared very thin in the sonograms, suggesting they came from one and not two eggs. I hadn't known this before, but genetics apparently *can* be involved when a mother produces an extra egg—yielding fraternal twins—but not when the egg splits in two. Identical twins, therefore, are no more than a fluke of nature, a random biological event.

We sat tight for four weeks after Kim's first doctor visit, trying not to be too excited or talk too much about the whole thing and waiting eagerly for the February appointment. Throughout Kim's short pregnancy, the time between doctor visits seemed to drag on forever. With every appointment we reached an important benchmark—twelve, sixteen, twenty weeks—or learned something new, such as the babies' genders or whether they were identical or fraternal twins.

We passed the time between doctor visits by keeping busy with work or around the house. We had bought an 1830s farmhouse at auction nearly two years before. The house, near the western edge of Virginia's Shenandoah Valley, is about a two-hour drive from Washington, D.C. For a couple of years before we bought it, we owned a cabin farther south in the valley. We were there as many weekends as we could be, and we fell head over heels in love with the area. It would get to Sunday night or, more frequently, Monday morning, and we were sick to leave and go back to the city. The open spaces reeled us in.

The farmhouse was definitely a "fix 'er upper," the kind of house you'd advertise as having "great potential," a clear indication that someone would be potentially crazy to buy it. But buy it we did. And, in the year and a half after the auction, we worked with a local contractor and on our own to get the place in shape—installing central heat, updating the electrical system, adding a bathroom and laundry, sanding and polishing the wide-board pine floors, exposing the interior log walls, patching the plaster where we could, and painting and painting and painting some more.

By the time Kim was pregnant, we were about through fixing up the front half of the house. We decided to put off doing a lot of work on the back half—kitchen and dining room downstairs, two vacant rooms above—until later, potentially much later. Money was an obvious issue, and there was really no rush. Besides, getting the rest of the house done was work enough.

We and our dog, Django, a shelty mix we picked up at the D.C. pound, moved permanently to the Shenandoah Valley from Washington in the fall after we bought the farmhouse. Within months, we had taken in two more mutts, Weber and Murphy, from the Shenandoah County shelter.

Kim and I had lived for six years in a one-bedroom D.C. condominium on Connecticut Avenue by the National Zoo. Now, instead of 900 square feet, we had more than double that on 17-plus acres, with wonderful mountain views and an old, red barn. There was even a two-hole outhouse.

The idea was that we would eventually use our land to start some sort of nursery business; Kim had recently completed her work toward a master's degree in horticulture from the University of Maryland. In the meantime, we planned to keep up the previous owner's practice of renting the land to two local farmers for pasture and for growing alfalfa, soybeans, and corn. While we were figuring out what we wanted to do, I would continue my consulting work, writing and editing speeches, publications, and other materials for various Washington-based nonprofit organizations and trade groups. My work required me to be in D.C. about two days a week on average, which I figured I could handle without a problem.

We hadn't thought seriously about children until a few months after the move, when we were settling into the house and the property and realizing it would be a wonderful place to have kids. They could run around in the fields, climb the tree in the yard, hide in the barn, raise animals, join the 4-H or the FFA, whatever.

Having kids was never a given for Kim and me. It was something we didn't really talk about for years—not because we were avoiding the issue, but because we felt it wasn't an option at the time. We had our one-bedroom condo and our dog, and there just wasn't room. And despite living in D.C.

for more than ten years, neither of us had ever felt completely settled there. Neither of us ever felt like it was home.

Besides, Kim and I both were in transitional periods in our lives. I was trying to find out if I could keep up a business of my own and still pay the bills. Kim was focused on getting her horticultural degree and starting a new life in gardening; she worked part-time and summers at various public gardens in and around D.C. Each of us, it seemed, wanted to answer a few more questions about life before we seriously addressed the question of kids.

The fact is, for a few years it seemed we were leaning pretty much against having kids. I had started to approach the issue from what I guess you'd call an existentialist point of view, thinking there really isn't much to life so who am I to inflict it on another, innocent being. For a time, I had thought it was presumptuous of parents to think they know what's best for these little creatures they bring into the world, to think that somehow everything will be different for their child, that he or she will live fulfilled. I remember reading a column in *Newsweek* by a woman who, with her husband, had decided not to have children. She was defending their decision as one that more couples should consider instead of parading blindly into parenthood. I remember agreeing with practically everything she wrote.

I remember thinking it's odd that people who decide to go childless often are tagged as selfish—they just don't want to be tied down, people reason—when it's those who *have* kids who are putting their own interests first. Again, it's this assumption that we have an inalienable right to bring another person into this world, to subject someone else to all the silliness and the uncertainty we face from day to day. It's not that I was suicidal, terminally depressed, or anything like that. I just felt that going to school and then working for the rest of your life didn't cut it as a reason for being. I was having enough trouble trying to justify my own existence. How could I justify someone else's?

But as we settled into a new life in the Shenandoah Valley, I finally started to feel that I was figuring things out, that I had a purpose. Kim and I had this great new home we were working on, making it more and more our own every day. We had fields and mountains and open sky all around. And we had a plan. We were finally in a place where we felt comfortable, where we were getting to know people, and where we could see ourselves staying for many years, a lifetime even.

I suddenly felt we had a life we'd be crazy not to share with children and that our children would be fortunate to have us as their parents and this place as their home. Kim agreed that the time had come. She was thirty-two, so we felt the sooner we got started the better.

Despite our newfound enthusiasm for making babies, our reservations about having children resurfaced from time to time even after we began to pursue our new objective. There was a month or so, when Kim and I were having a little trouble getting pregnant, when we just stopped trying. Suddenly, we were thinking all over again about why we were doing this. It seemed so unnatural—having to keep close track of Kim's temperature, sticking to a schedule for sex, and having to monitor my beer intake on the appointed evenings so we'd be sure I could "perform."

Part of me feels you should definitely have to work at something as important as having a child. But another part feels it should happen more naturally—that if you're meant to have kids you'll have kids. *It should just happen.* Having a bedside record of all the times we'd had sex over the last few months suddenly seemed too forced.

During our short break from regimented lovemaking, we even for a few days investigated the possibility of adopting. "Why not take care of a baby who's already in this world?" we wondered. "A baby who already needs someone's help?" That way, we'd never once have to face the guilt of having placed another human being on an unsympathetic planet. All we'd have to do would be to love the child, to provide, to give him or her a fighting chance.

The idea of adopting passed quickly, however, and Kim and I resumed our purposeful pursuit of pregnancy in November. It was early January when we found out we were having twins. Our initial anxieties aside, the outcome was almost too perfect—as if our decision to have children had been doubly affirmed.

At Kim's second checkup in February, both fetuses were still there in the ultrasound, but now the blobs of light were a little larger and had assumed an odd new shape, like peanuts in the shell. Kim was about nine weeks pregnant at the time, and we were planning to hold off on making her pregnancy public until she had one more appointment in early March. It still was hard to talk too much about the whole thing; we didn't want to get too excited. Any time we mentioned the possibility of twins, we reminded ourselves that it was still just that: a possibility.

I remember wondering how disappointed I'd be if we lost one of the little fetuses between checkups, if we suddenly learned we were having just one baby, if we were suddenly like most everyone else. I wondered if somehow it would affect our feelings about the pregnancy, about our baby. We may not have talked a lot about it, but like the fetuses inside Kim, the idea of twins had implanted itself in my brain and was growing there, assuming new shapes, new forms, and new potential with every passing day. I remember thinking that having just one baby now inevitably would be a letdown. We'd love the baby with all our hearts, of course, but there would always be a sense that we were denied this wonderful chance.

Shortly after I first learned Kim was pregnant with twins, I read that twins account for about one in ninety pregnancies in the United States. As our March appointment came closer, I held fast to the belief and the hope that Kim's pregnancy would be the one. I'd catch myself running, swimming, or driving and thinking of nothing but a long list of possible names for our babies. I regularly guessed at their genders, wondered who they'd be more like—me or Kim—and dreamed of driving through the Shenandoah Valley, just me and the twins, the three of us side by side in the bench seat of the used Ford pickup Kim and I had bought the year before.

Four

Our life at the UVA hospital quickly settled into a regimented routine. Kim was having her blood taken and tested every six hours and her vital signs monitored up to the minute. The idea was to catch her when she started falling, to move in the moment there was any sign that her condition was getting worse, and then to do the one thing that would make her better: deliver the twins.

Waiting for my wife to show signs that she was becoming perilously ill was about the weirdest experience I had ever had. The waiting was like a timeout, a period of eerie calm before our lives would be forever changed.

Throughout the night Tuesday, the nurse was in to check on Kim and to record her vital signs and the babies' heart rates every hour. The doctors had reassured us again and again that Kim's health was their top priority. All they were doing was buying precious time for the babies, giving them as strong a chance as possible before Kim's own health was at risk.

We would deliver, the doctors told us, at the first sign that Kim's condition was becoming more serious—when tests showed that her platelets were starting to drop or that her liver enzymes were on the rise. The doctors also were watching for physical cues, such as increased reflexes or additional swelling, that might suggest Kim was getting sicker. They'd come in on their rounds, tap at her knees and elbows with their little hammers, pull down the bed sheets to inspect her ankles for swelling, and then leave, only to return a few hours later.

In retrospect, the slow-but-certain swelling, or edema, that had started to announce itself over the previous two weeks in Kim's hands, feet, and face was a clear sign of the sickness that ultimately would end her pregnancy. Even the sharp pain Kim had felt in her right shoulder the week before could now be explained. As preeclampsia advances toward eclampsia and HELLP, the liver gets bigger, causing pain in the "right upper quadrant," according to the medical texts. But Kim hadn't even told her doctor about the shoulder pain, assuming it was run-of-the-mill soreness and that, together with the swelling, it was part of the price you pay for twins.

As we talked to the doctors and nurses during their regular visits to our room, it became clear that Kim's platelet count was the number everyone was watching the closest, and with good reason. If her platelets sank too low, Kim's blood would have trouble clotting once the doctors cut her open for the C-section. She'd just keep on bleeding, and the consequences could be disastrous.

Throughout Tuesday night and Wednesday, Kim's platelets held steady at a count of 100,000 or more per microliter of blood—still low compared to normal levels of 140,000 to 450,000, but an improvement over the initial reading Tuesday at the hospital in Winchester, where her count had been 75,000. Abnormal bleeding can occur when platelets drop below the 30,000 level, but clotting problems can start long before that. Consequently, the doctors told us they'd deliver our babies as soon as they saw Kim's platelets start to drop from the 100,000 range, primarily because there was no telling how low they'd go or how fast.

The platelet count is part of the most commonly performed blood test hospitals do, the complete blood cell count, or CBC. A basic analysis of the cellular components of the blood, a CBC measures the levels of red and white blood cells, in addition to the platelets.

Every time they drew Kim's blood for a CBC, we would wait anxiously for the test results. When we received word that there was no change in Kim's condition, we would breathe a short-lived sigh of relief, taking whatever pleasure we could in the fact that our babies now had at least several more hours to grow inside their mother.

Meanwhile, Kim's blood pressure had stabilized. At the doctor's office in Winchester on Tuesday, it was at 130/90. Throughout Tuesday night and Wednesday, her systolic pressure—the higher number that measures the pressure in the arteries when the heart is contracting—hovered in the 120s and 130s. Meanwhile, her diastolic pressure—the pressure when the heart is relaxed—was down in the 60s and 70s, occasionally even dipping into the 50s. The improvement in Kim's blood pressure was a likely, if temporary, result of the steroids she had been given to help the babies, the doctors said.

Wednesday, May 28, 1100: From time to time, I'll catch myself staring at the monitors like I'm watching TV. I'm transfixed. Now that we know what all the numbers mean, we follow them like hawks, keeping close track of the babies' heartbeats—still humming along in the 140s—or looking up every fifteen minutes when the cuff on Kim's arm pumps up automatically to measure her blood pressure. As long as we can see that the babies' hearts are still pumping away or that Kim's blood pressure is holding steady or going down, then we're reassured that all's well. At least for now.

Keeping track of the babies' heartbeats turned out to be a struggle. Just locating the smaller fetus, the one the doctors referred to as "Baby B," was causing enormous trouble for the nurses. With one fetal monitor held firmly in place on the lower left side of Kim's abdomen and picking up the steady clop-CLOP of Baby A's heart, the nurses would move the other monitor up and down and from side to side across Kim's belly in search of a second, distinct beat. At one point, they had to bring in a portable sonogram machine just to locate the little girl—not because they doubted she was there or because they thought there was a problem, but because she was just so damn hard to find. Inevitably, once they found her and placed the monitor just so, she was on the move a half hour or an hour later. Lost again.

Wednesday, May 28, 1430: She moves around in a game of prenatal hide-and-seek, from high up in Kim's belly to down low and back again. A precocious and playful little girl. We like that. Baby A, on the other hand, is always there, reliable and easy to find. Odd that we feel we are already beginning to get to know these little girls of ours.

By Wednesday afternoon, I was in the habit of making regular trips back and forth from the "nourishment room" across the hall. I'd get juice or ice water and maybe some crackers for me, and nothing but ice chips for Kim. She was under strict orders not to eat or even drink water, primarily because the doctors wanted to be sure she had an empty stomach if they decided to put her under general anesthesia for the operation. Another reason for Kim's fasting was the need to monitor as many of her vital functions as possible for clues that something might be awry. The fact that Kim wasn't consuming anything more substantial than ice chips enabled the doctors to track her fluid intake and urine output with battlefield precision.

From time to time, the nurses would empty the clear plastic receptacle that hung on a hook on the bottom of the bed collecting Kim's urine for all to see. Before disposing of its contents, they'd make note of the volume and then do a dip to measure the protein. On Wednesday, Kim's protein level was still on the high side of normal, but not as high as it had been in Winchester—again, a possible consequence of the steroid injections.

Kim hadn't eaten a thing since Tuesday morning and, by Wednesday afternoon, was becoming painfully hungry. She had been on an IV drip to meet her nutrition and hydration needs since she was first admitted to the hospital, but her stomach was crying out for something to eat and digest. I probably wasn't helping much, bringing up breakfast and then lunch from the hospital cafeteria and eating at her bedside. But the last thing I wanted to do was to leave Kim alone.

On Wednesday around midday came a reprieve: Kim's platelet count actually was on the rise, reaching 120,000 by noon and then 134,000 at the time of the 6:00 P.M. CBC. This didn't mean Kim had somehow been cured, they told us, just that she was not at great risk right then. Over the course of the day, the demeanor of the doctors and nurses became less urgent and dire. Starting after her 6:00 P.M. labs, the doctors ordered that blood tests be taken every twelve hours instead of every six. And the nurses went from checking Kim's vitals every hour to doing it every three hours.

The doctors assured us they still were certain the babies would have to be delivered soon, but it wasn't clear if that meant two days, several days, or more. Kim and I talked about having to be prepared for the inevitable rush of activity that would take over our now-quiet room when the time came to deliver. Nevertheless, we both wondered if maybe we could buy time until the babies' chances were more assured. On Wednesday night, one of the nurses suggested we could be there till the end of June. She said she'd seen it happen lots of times before. Granted, every doctor and nurse we had talked to until then had said it was a matter of days at best. But we were taking our encouragement wherever and from whomever we could find it.

Wednesday, May 28, 2000: You start to understand the incredible power these people have over your emotions. First you're

hearing you have days or just hours and then, all of a sudden,
someone opens the door to a whole new possibility: your babies
might indeed be born at twenty-eight weeks. You are fast to em-
brace any statement, theory, or turn of phrase that sounds even
remotely more optimistic than what you've heard before. I wonder
if the doctors and nurses know—really know—how much we hang
on their every word.

Once we had called our parents Wednesday afternoon to
give everyone an update, I took advantage of the break in the
action to go for a run around the UVA campus and buy flowers for our room. When I returned, a basket of yellow daisies
in hand, three white-coated doctors—all new faces—were
standing at Kim's bedside. They were from pediatrics, an attending physician and two residents, and they were there to
talk to us about what happens to preterm babies after they're
born.

The doctors acknowledged that twenty-four or twenty-five
weeks is very early, but they said there are plenty of cases
of "extremely premature" infants doing fine. They resisted
when I pressed them for hard numbers on survival rates—
something quantitative, something we could latch onto. All
they would say was that our babies had a fighting chance of
doing all right. "That's why we have a NICU," one of them
said, referring to the Newborn Intensive Care Unit on the
seventh floor.

I then asked the pediatricians what were some of the health
and developmental problems babies like ours can run into.
After remarking that every case is different and that there's
no telling what might happen, the doctors started through a
seemingly endless list of medical misfortune and trauma, from
blindness and deafness to cerebral palsy, brain bleeds, organ

malfunction, developmental retardation, and more. Before they could finish, Kim put up her hand.

"I've heard enough," she said. "Thank you very much, but I've heard enough."

Before the doctors left, one of them suggested I take a tour of NICU so at least one of us would know what to expect. Our nurse that day already had suggested this—she even offered to call down to the seventh floor and arrange the tour—but I had put her off. In the back of my mind, I was still hoping we had lots of time, that we'd be there a good while before we even had to think about the NICU. But now the tour sounded like a good idea.

Later in the evening while Kim slept, I took the elevator down a floor to the children's center on seven. Our nurse had called to make sure it was a good time to visit; she said to ask for Judy. I had no idea what to expect to see there. I had never thought much about premature infants before. Maybe I'd seen some pictures in a magazine once or twice, but I had no real sense of the size of these babies or how fully developed they were. Could you touch and hold them? I didn't even know.

I called into the NICU from the phone on the wall outside the door, and the receptionist buzzed it open. Judy was there to greet me within seconds. Standing behind me while I washed my hands at the scrub station and tied a blue gown around my neck and waist, Judy explained that UVA recently separated the very premature, very low-birth-weight babies from the rest of the NICU clientele—babies who are born closer to term but who have other complications, other problems. Judy said the NICU had two spaces set aside for our babies in the very low-birth-weight unit; she called it

"C-Pod." She said they were waiting for word from upstairs about Kim.

Knowing that the NICU was waiting for our babies suddenly made our delivery feel more imminent, more real than before. The idea that people were planning on it, that they had two spaces already set aside, was startling. It cracked a hole in the wall of denial that I had built up over the course of the afternoon as Kim's condition improved.

It is often said that a parent's first visit to the NICU is a blur of machines, lights, and alarms. But as Judy and I rounded the corner into C-Pod, all I could focus on were the babies—tiny, fragile, alien-like beings with out-of-proportion heads and red, translucent skin hanging loose on their little bones. They were lying completely naked in their open beds, a tangle of wires, tubes, and IVs extending in all directions from their too-little bodies.

Judy invited me to stand at the bedside of one of the five or six infants in the pod. It was a boy. He was curled up tight on his elbows and knees, the red oximeter light on his foot bathing his tiny, wrinkled rear end in an otherworldly glow. Balled up like he was, I figured he was about the size of a cantaloupe, maybe smaller. Judy said he had been born at twenty-four weeks gestation and was now about two weeks old.

As we stood over his bed, Judy was talking to me—I'm sure about the technology and the care these babies get—but I wasn't really listening. My eyes filled to the brink with tears that I tried in vain to blink away. I couldn't imagine that our babies would end up like this—so vulnerable, so desperate-looking, so incomplete.

Back in our room upstairs, Kim asked about the tour. I told her the nurses all seemed like wonderful people. I said I was impressed. This was a stupid and evasive answer, of course, but I didn't want to get into any more detail. I didn't want to scare Kim with descriptions of the babies and how small they were. I didn't want to, that is, until Kim asked the question flat out.

"What do the babies look like?" she asked.

"They're small," I said.

"Like how small?" she asked.

"Real small," I said.

That was the end of the conversation. I don't think Kim wanted to pursue it any further, and I knew I didn't. We'd just wait and see, I thought. Talking to my parents on the phone a little later, I finally broke down. After I told them I had taken the tour, my mom asked what the babies looked like. I took a deep breath before answering. "They're so small," I said, almost whispering, and in a second tears were streaming from my eyes. I told my parents to hold on, and I put down the phone and wiped my eyes and nose on the sleeve of my shirt like a little boy at school.

During our hospital stay and the months that followed, I learned that it is often more difficult to talk about what you're going through than simply to live it. The whole time we were in the hospital, Kim couldn't get on the phone without shaking. It was as if in committing our experience and our feelings to words, it made them real. You start telling what's happened, telling your story, and you can hardly believe it's you talking. You can hardly believe it's all true.

When I put the phone back to my ear, I told my parents I was sorry. I told them I hadn't had enough sleep the night before, trying for whatever reason to discount my emotions, to attribute my behavior to something other than the outright terror of our situation.

My parents, as usual, were enormously supportive. "Don't be sorry," they said. "There's no reason to be sorry."

Wednesday, May 28, 2230: Medical students probably tour these units all the time with an exhilarated detachment, fascinated that we have the technology and the know-how to save babies who would otherwise be dead. But it's so amazingly different when it's happening to you. There is no detachment. There can't be. Today I am imagining returning to the NICU to stand helpless at our babies' bedsides while the nurses do their work. And I am imagining wondering how it came to be that we were denied the chance to have normal, healthy twins.

Five

When Kim called from the doctor's office to say that her March ultrasound confirmed she was still pregnant—and still with twins—I could hardly contain myself. Before Kim even made it home that morning, I had called several friends, my brothers, my uncles. When I told people I had news, I'm sure they all had an idea what it was. Virtually all of our married friends had one or two babies by then, and they were always asking when we'd be having kids ourselves.

The news that we were having two babies, however, was a 100 percent certifiable surprise. "Twins, my God, I don't believe it," they said. Everyone I spoke with said it was wonderful news, although they all joked in various ways that Kim and I would have our hands full, that our lives would be forever changed. People were genuinely excited for us. And their excitement fanned my own.

With every phone call, I became more fired up about Kim's pregnancy, more possessive of this unique and wonderful thing that was happening in my life, more proud. It was as if in making the pregnancy public, I was making it real. Before it had been almost entirely in my head, but now I could talk about it. Now I could give it shape and form. Now I could unveil it, like a work of art I was dying to show the world.

Two telephone calls that Kim and I were not excited about making were to Kim's pregnant sister, Kris, and to our close friends, Bob and Teri, who had found out recently—once and for all—that they couldn't have kids. The issue with Kris was the standard sibling stuff: Here she was, having the first grandchild in the family, and we were jumping into the spotlight with our announcement of twins.

With Bob and Teri, the issues were much more complicated. This was a couple that had gone to enormous lengths over several years to try to have a child. Teri even ended up in the hospital for several days because of an adverse reaction to fertility treatments that in the end were unsuccessful. Now they were trying to adopt. They'd had a home visit from the adoption agency and now were putting together a color brochure for prospective birth parents outlining who they were, why they wanted a child, and how much love they had to give.

I called Bob to meet him for lunch on one of my days in the city. I told him our news over a sandwich and chips at an outdoor table on K Street in downtown D.C. The four of us were planning a trip to Key West later in March, and I suppose Kim and I could have waited to tell Bob and Teri while we were there. But for whatever reason, we felt that Teri needed to know, that she needed to understand before we all went that she'd be spending several days in the Keys with a pregnant friend. That evening, Bob took flowers home and told Teri our news.

"It's hard," he told me at lunch, obviously excited that we were expecting, but at the same time concerned about how Teri might react. "A lot of our friends are suddenly having babies, and it's hard," he said.

Watching two of our closest friends deal with the torment of infertility at the precise time that Kim had become pregnant reminded us to take nothing for granted. We may have been ambivalent about having children just months before, but we couldn't be ambivalent now. It wouldn't be fair. How many couples, we wondered, were out there trying in vain to get pregnant? How many were there like Bob and Teri who always imagined they would have their own children and who now knew they would not? How many would say we were blessed?

As our Florida trip approached, we began to wonder if Kim could make it. February had been a rough month. It seems I awoke every morning to the sound of her heaving in the bathroom. Kim had heard from her doctor and others that morning sickness can be worse with twins, and now she was learning this unpleasant fact firsthand. Early in the pregnancy, she found out that whenever she became hungry, she got sick. To keep her stomach busy through the night, Kim kept a Ziplock bag of graham crackers and Saltines on the table by the bed.

If heaves were the sound of the morning during the first trimester of Kim's pregnancy, then the noise of the night was the crunching of crackers. I'd wake up, roll over, and see Kim sitting up in the dark and stuffing crackers in her mouth like an automaton, taking no pleasure in the taste of the things, just wanting to get them down.

Kim kept up her practice of walking in the morning, but she wasn't getting out of the house until later and later as February wore on. She had to wait until she felt better and was confident she wouldn't get sick.

But by mid-March Kim was feeling a lot better. The big joke was that Bob and I had booked the rooms in Key West— European-style, with several rooms sharing a toilet. This at a time when my wife was using the toilet several times a day for purposes other than the normal ones. The only other option in the inn where we wanted to stay was an apartment-style setup with two rooms, living room and bath. But that would have cost us considerably more.

"And besides," I told Kim, "there's a sink in the room. You can use the sink."

This did not make me very popular in our household. Fortunately for both of us, Kim had to use the sink to heave just once or twice over the course of our four days in Key West. It was hard to believe she had been so sick for so many weeks. Driving from Miami down the overseas highway to the Keys, Bob, Teri, Kim, and I ate almost all the rice cakes Kim had brought to keep her stomach happy and quiet between meals. She didn't need them anymore.

The main activity in Key West was meals out. It was spring break, so the main drag, Duvall Street, was bustling all night. With the help of the staff at the inn, we found a couple of out-of-the-way places for dinner—a little nouveau Italian bistro on a quiet residential block of colorful Key West Victorian homes and a place with a huge brick patio where we listened to acoustic music by candlelight and enjoyed the best meal of the trip. During the daytime, we poked in and out of the shops, hung around the hotel pool, played tennis, took a tour of the Hemingway House, and chartered a sailboat that took us out into the shallows, where we kayaked through mangrove islands and snorkeled. A couple of nights after dinner, Bob, Teri, and I went out for drinks without Kim. That and the raw oysters were the only things she missed.

It was a wonderful trip, and while the four of us often discussed the finer points of pregnancy, adoption, twins, and all the rest, I never felt we were obsessing about it. There were plenty of other things to talk about and do. We left Bob and Teri on a Tuesday morning to drive about six hours north on the Atlantic Coast for a visit with my parents in their winter home at Vero Beach. Bob and Teri were staying a little longer in the Keys and then driving to the Everglades and up the Gulf Coast to sightsee and play golf.

Back home after our week in the Florida sun, we anxiously awaited Kim's early-April doctor's appointment, when we hoped we'd find out the genders of our babies. I don't know exactly why, but in the back of my mind I always expected girls. Kim said she felt the same way. As the middle child of three boys, I think I was secretly hoping for girls, for something different. I also wanted girls for Kim's sake. My wife is the oldest of three girls. Boys, I thought, she would never understand.

The appointment at 3:00 P.M. on Wednesday, April 2 marked my first visit to Kim's doctor. It was an important one, with another ultrasound planned and the likelihood we'd learn the babies' genders. As Kim's pregnancy progressed, it was becoming more and more apparent that the number of ultrasounds we were seeing was a real luxury; other pregnant couples we knew were forced to wait until the fourth or fifth month for their first look at their baby. But the doctors watch you more closely when you're having twins, and so you get to see for yourself how the little ones are growing. We were in the twentieth week and already we'd seen two sets of pictures.

We have eight ultrasound printouts from the April 2 checkup—a clear indication that Kim's doctor was taking her time with us and having fun. There a beautiful nose-up profile of one of the babies; a shot from the bottom of a pair of teeny feet, like footprints on the moon; and an amazing full body profile, the baby's back arched, its ribs cutting straight lines up and down through the center of the print. Dr. O'Bannon identified the fetuses as A and B, and already it appeared that one was bigger than the other. She used the machine to measure the circumferences of the babies' heads, among other body parts. Her conclusion: Baby B was a few days behind.

"Nothing to worry about right now," she said. "We'll just keep an eye on it."

The net effect of the ultrasound images was a picture in my mind of two little creatures—little *humans*—separated only by a thin membrane that they were constantly reaching across. Prodding, poking, kicking, and caressing. The images made me wonder if our babies were in some way aware that they had company. Did they know they weren't alone?

It was remarkable to me that all of this was going on in my wife's belly. Apart from a few flutters now and then, she couldn't even feel it yet. It was like a hidden circus no one knew about, out in the woods somewhere or underground. And all the people and all the animals were performing and doing their tricks, but there was no one there to watch.

We asked Dr. O'Bannon if she could tell the babies' genders.

"You really want to know?" she asked.

We both nodded our heads yes, having decided we'd want to be as ready as possible, with the proper clothes and everything else, when the babies came home. Moreover, the idea of five to six more months of guesswork struck us both as torture.

"Well, I don't see anything that would suggest they're boys," Dr. O'Bannon told us. "I probably won't be able to tell you for sure until next time, but it looks like you'll be having little girls." Dr. O'Bannon also said she suspected they were identical, considering the thinness of the membrane between them.

Identical twin girls—like in *The Shining*. I could hardly believe it. Leaving Dr. O'Bannon's office, I noticed Kim was a little quiet. "What's up?" I asked. "Aren't you excited about the girls?"

She said she was, but she was concerned about the smaller size of Baby B.

"But Dr. O'Bannon says it's not a problem. So don't worry about it. We'll see how she's doing next time."

We had deliberately scheduled an ultrasound appointment for the very end of April, just to make sure they both were growing all right. That would still give us a chance to do an amniocentesis if we noticed a problem. Although we weren't sure what we'd do, we felt we wanted to give ourselves every opportunity to know what we were dealing with, what to expect. And Dr. O'Bannon assured us she could tell a lot from an ultrasound.

That night I called my parents to give them the news. Dad was home; Mom, he told me, was with my Uncle Michael and his two daughters in Massachusetts. Michael was dying of cancer; he had been sick for a number of years. He was my mother's youngest brother—fifty-four years old when he died—and we were all quite close. As a child, I was regularly told that I looked like Michael. Even into my twenties, my grandfather often made the mistake of calling me "Mike" without even realizing he was wrong.

Michael had introduced my two brothers and me to Bob Dylan, the Everly Brothers, and Buddy Holly. He was more like an older sibling than an uncle. The day I first heard he had cancer was the only time I had cried in years. Michael had stoked my enduring passion for rock and roll, folk, and country music, and I had always appreciated his absurd sense of humor. When I was away at boarding school and college, Michael and I regularly exchanged postcards and letters that were chock-full of jokes and moronic commentary on items in the news.

Michael was divorced and single, a professor at Williams College in the western part of Massachusetts. Apart from Christmases at my parents' house in Pennsylvania, he and I hadn't been in touch a whole lot since I first heard he was sick and likely to die. I had sent him a tape or two of some of my favorite recent songs, and we exchanged an occasional e-mail recommending CDs we'd bought, but the fact is I wasn't sure if I *wanted* to be in touch with Michael a whole lot in those final months and years. All I kept hearing from my parents and others in the family was that he was horribly depressed. My natural inclination was to stay away. My mother and her other siblings, I figured, were help enough for him. And I imagined him tiring of the family, tiring of people always inquiring about how he was doing, how he *felt*.

In February, Kim and I had gone to the wedding of Michael's youngest daughter in Connecticut. Cathleen and her fiancé had planned to be married that spring, but they wanted to make absolutely sure Michael could make it, so they moved up the date. When I first saw him that weekend, I was stunned at how old Michael looked. I could hardly say hello. He was thin, bald, weak, and walking on a cane.

Talking with my father on the phone about what Kim and I had learned at our April 2 doctor's appointment, I asked if he thought I should call my mother at Michael's to tell her our twins were girls. Michael wasn't doing very well, my father said. He said it might cheer everybody up if I called with our news.

Michael's older daughter, Sophie, answered and got my mom. When I asked what she thought of granddaughters, Mom was ecstatic. "You mean identical girls. I don't believe it," she said. I told her all about the appointment that day, and she suggested she put Michael on. "He's not doing too well," she whispered. "You should say hi."

When Michael got on the phone, his voice was so weak I could hardly tell what he was saying. "Michael," I said, "I'm having two girls, just like you." I told him I hoped they turned out as great as his two girls. Then he said something I didn't understand, and I laughed because most of the things Michael said were funny.

It was the last time I talked to my Uncle Mike; he died the following weekend. I already missed him when I hung up the phone.

The end of April is around the time that Kim's pregnancy started to become very real. We started once-a-week parenting classes at the local hospital. Kim was showing and getting larger, it seemed, by the day. Another sonogram confirmed that the fetuses indeed were girls and still were growing as they should. One was still a bit smaller, but Dr. O'Bannon assured us this was normal and shouldn't be a problem.

Before May, we hadn't done a whole lot of reading about what we were getting into. Kim was making her way through *What to Expect When You're Expecting*, but that was about it. I think Kim, in particular, felt we would somehow be jinxing ourselves by getting too excited and too invested too early. In D.C. for a weekend with friends in late April, she ran into a former coworker who she knew had been pregnant and due earlier in the year. Kim asked how the baby was, and the woman told her they had to terminate the pregnancy at six months after an ultrasound showed severe problems. "It makes you wonder," Kim said.

Kim's reluctance to assume that her pregnancy would go the distance seemed to wane a bit after the late-April sonogram. Typically, she was extremely conscientious about finding the right books and magazines, the right people to talk to, the right ideas for everything from breastfeeding to setting up the nursery. She called a national association of mothers of twins, a local twin support group, and even a breastfeeding specialist in Winchester who was a mother of older twins. We started to get more mail on the subject—subscription mailers from *Twins Magazine*, membership information from various twin and parent groups, even a brochure about a twin crib Kim had seen advertised in the *Washington Post*.

We were beginning to amass a tremendous library of books and magazines and clipped-out articles on childbirth and twins—everything we needed to know and more. We even watched a Discovery Channel special that highlighted the unique, almost metaphysical bond between twins and showcased identicals as the focus of reams of fascinating research on human genetics—what's innate and what's learned. We were in deep. And the fact is, we weren't alone.

Throughout April and May, our families became increasingly invested in our pregnancy, too. Kim's mother, visiting in April, brought us an embarrassingly large wardrobe of adorable baby outfits, many of them in sets of two. She also came bearing loads of other gifts, everything from a diaper bag to stuffed animals, books, booties, and even baby lotion and shampoo. Our dining room table was piled high with baby things shortly after Laura arrived. A little embarrassed at how much there was, Kim quickly set to the task of putting everything away upstairs.

My mother, for her part, was constantly asking what she could do for us. "What do you need?" she'd say. "We'll get you anything you need." When at first I couldn't tell her exactly what we needed—we were still thinking about it ourselves, still weighing all the dizzying options for cribs, car seats, strollers, and the rest—she told me to go out and buy an air conditioner for Kim. She was appalled, I think, that we were about to welcome the hot Virginia summer without anything more than a window fan to keep Kim cool.

It wasn't until Kim's father and his wife visited from Boston the third weekend in May that we started thinking seriously about larger baby purchases. Jim and Cynthia apparently had it in their minds that a major reason for their visit was to take us to the baby store and to help us start loading up on what we'd need. Although Kim was still a little scared to commit and to start spending significant amounts of money—even if it was somebody else's—she and I had recently embraced the theory that we wouldn't want to be shopping for baby things through the summer and that it would be best to get most everything done before Kim entered her potentially tortuous final weeks.

Jim and Cynthia insisted we go shopping with them during their visit, so we went to the Baby Depot store near the airport on Sunday afternoon. We weren't in the store for more than a half hour before we had a flatbed cart piled high with large boxes. Inside were two infant swings, two car seats, a twin stroller, a port-a-crib, even a dresser-top changing pad. Apart from two full-sized cribs, which Kim and I decided we'd buy later, we had found virtually all the big things we were talking about getting, everything we felt we needed. We never imagined getting it all at once.

Outside the store, the salesman helped us load everything into our Subaru station wagon. After several attempts, we finally got all the big boxes to fit. To mark the occasion, we took pictures of the four of us and the salesman standing around the car, all of us with goofy smiles that signaled something special was going on: Kim and I were having twins.

It was just nine days later that Kim entered the hospital, her twin pregnancy soon to end.

Six

Sitting in our hospital room Wednesday evening, Kim talked about how frustrating and how confusing it all was—not just to be in the hospital and not able to eat or get out of bed, but to have everyone telling you that you're gravely ill when you wouldn't even know it yourself. And, on top of that, to be sitting there and knowing that there are things going on inside your body, things you can't control, that might harm you and your babies.

Kim remarked that she had an idea now how my uncle Michael must have felt about the cancer that had killed him earlier that spring. How powerless. How weak. How unable to do anything to stop the disease that was taking his life. And inevitably wondering if there was something he did to bring it on. In Kim's case, it was a big bag of potato chips we had shared on the drive home from our Memorial Day visit with my parents that became a possible culprit.

"They were so salty," she said, suggesting that the salt may have caused her blood pressure to rise.

"I don't think it was the potato chips," I replied.

Wednesday night was a particularly long one, not necessarily because we couldn't sleep, but because Kim became severely constipated. During the afternoon, after Kim's test results showed some improvement in her condition, the doctors had said she'd probably be able to eat something soon, although they didn't specify when. When we asked our day nurse about it around dinnertime, she returned with a prepackaged pita sandwich—broccoli—that she retrieved from the refrigerator in the nourishment room across the hall.

Within an hour or two after eating the sandwich, Kim was feeling gassy and bloated. Later that night, after we had turned down the lights to try and get some sleep, she said she could no longer stand it; she had to get up and go to the bathroom. I was sleeping when Kim pressed the call button, and I awoke to see our night nurse unplugging the blood pressure cuff and the monitors and rerigging the IVs so she could carry them with Kim across the room. I jumped up to help, but had to sit down again because I was dizzy from too little sleep. And so I watched from my bed as Kim waddled slowly and deliberately toward the bathroom, leaning hard on the nurse's shoulder and with the urine catheter dangling between her legs. In just thirty-six hours, I realized, she had turned into an invalid, an old woman.

Thursday, May 29, 0700: This is a woman who makes her own dresses; cans her own tomatoes, pickles, and beans; and who won't call a plumber, a contractor, or an electrician until she's absolutely convinced it's a job we can't handle ourselves. I can only imagine how enormously frustrating it is for her to be laid up like this—unable even to go to the bathroom without someone's help.

Once in the bathroom, Kim stayed there for more than a half hour, but she couldn't go. When she called out to say she was done, I went to find the nurse and we helped Kim back to her bed. While we were rerigging the IVs and the monitors, the nurse suggested in passing that a broccoli sandwich on an empty stomach was probably not the best thing for Kim to eat. I wondered about the stress to Kim's system and whether it might cause any problems and somehow accelerate the course of her illness. The whole idea, as I understood it, was for Kim to stay in bed, to stay rested and unstressed. But the gas and the pains had clearly shaken her up.

Before going back to sleep, Kim threw up into a bedpan that I held against her neck. The degree to which they felt they had to monitor Kim for any sign of trouble became clear when the nurse insisted on measuring the amount of vomit—50 cc.

Later, after sleeping another hour or so, Kim again pressed the call button for the nurse. She said she was desperate to go to the bathroom; the pain was too intense. It was a little before six o'clock in the morning when the nurse gave Kim a suppository. Then, around eight o'clock, they tried an enema, and it worked. Kim was in the bathroom within minutes. She hadn't slept much all night, but she said she was feeling better nonetheless.

The nurse had drawn blood for Kim's labs at 6:40 A.M. on Thursday. Once we had resolved the issue of getting Kim to the bathroom, I took a shower and went to the cafeteria to get breakfast and a newspaper. Meanwhile, we had checked again with the doctors about Kim's eating, and they suggested we order her a light breakfast from the hospital meal service—a muffin or oatmeal and juice. Kim's breakfast had been delivered by the time I returned, and we ate together at the table that extended over her bed. I then sat with a cup of coffee, reading my paper, while Kim went back to sleep.

When the nurse came in to check on Kim around ten o'clock, I asked about the results of the morning labs. We had been trying for two days to get the doctors and nurses on a schedule of telling us as soon as possible about the test results. It was futile. With all the shift changes and all the different personalities involved, it was never quite clear who was responsible for even finding out the test results, let alone communicating them to us. Nevertheless, we found that if we kept asking, we usually knew the results within a couple of hours. It wasn't that we didn't trust the doctors and nurses to have the results in enough time to do something if there was a problem. This was a hospital, after all, and we assumed they had fairly efficient systems for reporting and tracking all this stuff. We just wanted to know Kim was all right.

On Thursday morning, however, our nurse said she hadn't

heard anything yet. It was already more than three hours after they drew blood. She said she'd check on it.

After the nurse left, I noticed that Kim was dabbing at her nose with a tissue.

"Bloody nose?" I asked.

"It's no big deal," she said. "I think it's just dry in here."

I could see that the tissue was spotted very lightly with blood. "I guess you're right," I said.

I was reading and Kim was dozing off again when there was a faint knock on our door around eleven o'clock. Looking up from my book, I saw Kim's father peering into the room with a big, silly smile on his face. "Surprise," he whispered, seeing Kim asleep. He explained that he'd been home in Cambridge early that morning walking his dog and decided he wanted to be with us. He got on the earliest flight to Charlottesville, and here he was.

In telephone conversations over the previous two days, all of our parents had asked if we felt we needed anyone with us in Charlottesville. My answer to everyone had been no. The whole idea, I explained, was to reduce the level of activity around Kim. I didn't want her stressed any more than she had to be. I didn't want her to have to worry about anyone but herself. Having two or three people sitting in our hospital room would be too much. I thought the quiet was good. And everyone seemed to understand.

Seeing Kim's dad, however, was an enormous relief. The quiet in our room may have been good, but it had become stifling over the previous two days. Just having someone else to talk to would be a good thing, I realized. Kim and I had talked and cried about as much as we could by then. All we could do now was wait.

After an extended round of hugs and kisses, Kim's father

pulled a chair up alongside Kim's bed and we all talked. We explained to him how all the monitors worked, what the different IVs were, and how the nurses still were having trouble finding Baby B on the fetal monitor. Kim's father said it sounded like the little girl had an attitude. "A lot like her mother," he said with a smile.

Around 11:30, I noticed Kim was dabbing again at her nose, and it looked to me like she was getting blood—not spotting, but blood.

"Is your nose still bleeding?" I asked.

She held up the tissue—dark red splotches. Kim suggested I shouldn't worry about it. "The nurse will be in again soon," she said. But I told her it probably wasn't a good thing to be bleeding like that, considering everyone's concern about the platelets and her blood's ability to clot.

When I went outside to tell the nurse, she asked if Kim's nose was really bleeding, if I was really seeing blood. I told her I was, and she said she'd be in our room in a minute. At the time, it didn't occur to me that we still hadn't heard about the results of the morning blood test.

Shortly after I was back in the room, the nurse knocked and entered; we could see several people in the hallway before she closed the door behind her. I looked at Kim and she at me, the blank expressions on our faces indicating we both knew what was up. This was it. It all was happening now. I looked at the clock on the wall above the television. It was 11:45, just fifteen minutes shy of the forty-eight hours they told us we needed for the steroids to kick in and strengthen the babies' lungs, for the girls to have that much more of a chance.

Our nurse explained in a rush that Kim's blood results had come back and that it was time to operate. She then went back and opened the door. In an instant, there were seven or eight other people in our room, working furiously to unhook Kim from her monitors, move the IVs, and transfer her to a stretcher they had wheeled in from the hallway outside. Jim and I stepped back from the bed so we weren't in the way. One of the doctors, an anesthesiologist, asked when Kim last ate. We told him about her breakfast. Another held a sheet of paper in front of her explaining the risks of C-section. She asked Kim to sign it.

It all was happening too fast. Just as we expected. Just as we knew it would. As they wheeled Kim out of our room for the quick trip down the hall to the operating room, I kissed her on the forehead and told her I'd see her there. Kim didn't say a word.

Seven

I wasn't there to see our babies come into the world. Neither was Kim, really. The picture-perfect, 1990s delivery, with the mother awake and alert and the father on hand to share in the moment while offering whatever emotional support he can, was not to be ours.

In their rush to the operating room with my wife, the doctors had told me to suit up in surgical scrubs in case they decided on a regional injection, or epidural. If Kim was going to be awake for the delivery, they said it wouldn't be a problem for me to be there. If she was asleep, however, I'd have little to do besides get in the way.

In the end, the doctors decided to put her to sleep. Apparently, their interest in moving fast and efficiently outweighed their fear that Kim might aspirate the breakfast she'd eaten just a couple of hours before. The fact that the doctors had allowed Kim to eat that morning—knowing full well that they would probably want to put her under when the time came to deliver—was a reminder that they were as unprepared as we for Kim's all-too-sudden decline.

Not being in the operating room was perfectly fine with me. I had always planned to be on hand for our babies' birth, but that was before we knew they'd be born under such stressful and potentially gory conditions. Fact is, I was almost relieved when the nurse came back and told me they were putting Kim to sleep and that I'd have to wait in our room with Kim's dad. As I took off the scrubs I had thrown on in a rush, I only regretted that I hadn't said anything more meaningful to Kim on her way out the door.

It was a little after noon when Kim's father and I finally were left alone to wait. After the hurricane of activity, our hospital room was strangely, hauntingly silent. The monitors that had kept us so engaged over the previous two days had all been turned off. The clop-CLOP-clop-CLOP-clop-CLOP of our babies' heartbeats was gone. Kim's bed sat up empty, the sheets and blankets all rumpled and in a pile to remind us of her hasty exit.

It's all pretty much of a fog, but I remember that Jim and I both were having trouble sitting down. I remember the two of us walking back and forth across the room from time to time and taking pains to stay out of each other's way. Before long, I decided I'd eat the turkey sandwich they had brought Kim for lunch just a few minutes before she was wheeled out the door.

"Good thing she didn't eat that," I told Jim, trying to make conversation. I offered him half the sandwich. He declined.

Jim and I didn't talk a whole lot while we were waiting. What was there to say? But having him there was an enormous relief. A former Harvard economics professor who left the university to head a Cambridge policy institute, Jim had in recent years become an avid sailor. Among his prize possessions is a 40-foot boat he keeps in Maine. Kim and I had been sailing there with Jim and his wife, Cynthia, two summers before, and the four of us had recently chartered a boat in the Virgin Islands with Cynthia's two sons. Kim and I also tried to make a habit of visiting Jim and Cynthia at their weekend home in Gloucester, Massachusetts, at least once or twice a year. We got to love the area so much while we were dating that we decided to get married there.

The four of us had always gotten along more as friends than as family. We genuinely had a good time when we were together, in large part because Jim always insisted on it. Twenty-five years his junior, I regularly had found it a challenge to keep up with the man, whether we were running on the beach in Gloucester or drinking margaritas as the sun set over a craggy Caribbean island. Waiting quietly in our hospital room while my wife gave birth to our daughters down the hall, I couldn't imagine not having him there. I couldn't imagine being there alone.

The door to our room was open to the hall while Jim and I waited. Every once in awhile, we saw a nurse or doctor pass by in scrubs—our room was immediately adjacent to the doorway that connected the labor and delivery area to the operating room. I remember making note of the speed with which the people moved outside our door. The faster they were moving, the more I wondered if there was a problem. No one, it seemed, was moving slowly.

After awhile, I got Jim and me Cokes from the nourishment room across the hall. Outside in the nursing area, all was quiet; I assumed most everyone was with Kim. Jim and I wondered out loud what it meant that it was getting close to one o'clock and no one had come to talk to us. We both were inclined to look on the bright side; no one had given us any reason to think Kim was in any real danger. But after everything else that had happened to us over the previous two days, it was harder now to exile bad thoughts from my mind. I imagined Kim dying and the babies going on to live. I imagined all three of them dying. What would I do?

I wondered about the fact that it had been more than five hours since Kim's blood was drawn that morning. What if her platelets had been in a freefall all this time and they'd only just found out? What if they had waited too long? The doctors and nurses had taken great care of us over the preceding forty-eight hours, but I wondered how the hospital could screw up so badly.

Also on my mind was the broccoli sandwich Kim had eaten the night before. I felt paranoid thinking about something so stupid and so seemingly harmless—a broccoli sandwich of all things—but I found it hard to divorce Kim's sudden decline from the fact that she was up most of the night with gas pains. And I wondered if perhaps our nurse hadn't checked with the doctors and had gotten Kim something to eat—anything— just to shut us up about how hungry Kim was.

Finally, a little after one o'clock, one of the nurses came in and said everything was all right. The babies had been delivered and were put on ventilators, and Kim was OK. She said Jim and I could wait in a short hallway on the other side of the operating room to see the babies on their way to the NICU.

Peering through the window of a rolling incubator was not how I imagined I would first set eyes on our twins, but I was eager to see them just the same. When I asked the nurse how big they were and she answered 1 pound 6 ounces and 1 pound 2 ounces, I didn't even know what to say. Strangely, all I could think of were the $1^1/_2$-pound lobsters we used to bring home squirming from the seafood store during family vacations in Cape Cod. I imagined our babies fitting on a dinner plate. It's absurd the things that can enter your mind.

After the nurse left, Jim enveloped me in a big bear hug. "Congratulations, you're a father," he said.

"Thanks," I said, my eyes wet with tears. "I guess I am."

Jim and I waited in the hallway outside the operating room for ten or fifteen minutes; it seemed like hours. When the double doors from the operating room finally opened wide, a parade of eight doctors and nurses—four surrounding each incubator—pushed through with our babies. Everyone was still wearing surgical masks and scrubs. It was a shock to see so many people, a jolting reminder of our babies' critical condition. And yet it was reassuring to know that there was so much shared responsibility for their care. Later, we found out there had been as many as thirteen people on hand in the operating room for the delivery—a small army of surgeons, anesthesiologists, pediatricians, nurses, and who knows who.

A woman in the group with the first incubator called out to Jim and me as the parade moved briskly down the hall: "Are you the daddy of these beautiful girls?"

"Yes, I am," I said, my eyes welling up again.

The procession stopped in front of us for just a few seconds so we could look at the babies. One after the other, I bent over and quickly spoke my first words to our girls through their incubators' plastic shields. "Hi little girl. How you doin'?" In an instant, they were wheeled through the double doors to the elevator for the ride downstairs.

They were gone as if in a dream, but I remember being surprised at how *human* our babies looked—they had hands and feet, even hair. Their skin was bright red and everything was tiny, but I was relieved that it was all there. Everything was there. Only their faces were obscured by the tape holding the ventilator tubes in their tiny mouths.

"They *are* beautiful," I said to Jim after they left.

"Yes, they are," he said. He patted me on the back. Jim, too, later told me he was surprised they looked so human and so real. He said he hadn't known what to expect and was relieved. We hear that a baby will be born extremely premature, and we expect her to be malformed in some way, when the truth is she's just fragile and small. Very small.

The surgeon's official report on the delivery of our twins suggests it was a smooth, if bloody, procedure:

The patient was taken to the operating room where she was prepped and draped sterilely. General anesthesia was administered and a vertical skin incision was made from the umbilicus down to 2 cm above the pubic bone. . . . A vertical uterine incision was made from near the top of the uterus down to within 4 or 5 cm of the cervix. This was carried down through the myometrium until the placenta was reached. . . . A bulging endometrial amniotic sac was visualized and was sharply entered releasing clear fluid. The first twin was delivered vertex very easily and the cord was clamped, cut, and the baby was handed off the operative field to the pediatricians. The second baby was palpated and the amniotic bag was brought up to the uterine incision and ruptured as well with the release of clear fluid. The vertex was delivered as well as the remainder of the baby's body without any difficulty and the cord was clamped and cut and the baby was handed off to the pediatricians in the delivery room. The placenta was then delivered completely after cord sections were obtained for cord gas. . . . The uterus was bleeding somewhat heavily and at this point platelets were sent for and one unit of blood was infused. The uterus was then closed in four layers. . . . The abdomen was copiously irrigated and the uterus was found to be hemostatic at this point. . . . The skin was then closed with staples. . . . The patient was then extubated and sent to the recovery room in excellent condition. A total of 2 units of red blood cells were infused as well as 6 units of platelets and 2 units of fresh frozen plasma. The patient did tolerate the procedure well and there were no complications.

No complications, that is, apart from the need for a copious amount of blood products. We later learned that Kim's platelet count had dropped to 45,000 at the time of the delivery. In addition to the nose bleed she'd had earlier in the morning, bleeding was observed from the IV sites on her arms, further proof that her blood's ability to clot was in decline. The labs that were taken at 6:40 that morning—more than five hours before the operation—showed her platelets at 83,000, so they had been dropping fast. The combination of the infused platelets and the frozen plasma—the liquid part of the blood—helped stanch the bleeding and no doubt saved Kim's life.

As for the babies, the pediatrician's reports provide an insight into the frenzy of activity that took place off to the side of the room once our girls, referred to as "Baby Girl A" and "Baby Girl B," were born. Baby Girl A, whom we had known as "Baby B" in the sonograms, was the smaller of the two at 500 grams, or just over 1 pound. She apparently had the more stressful start, primarily because of problems the doctors had threading the ventilator's endotracheal tube down her tiny throat in a procedure called intubation.

Baby Girl A appeared "small, blue, and floppy" upon delivery, according to the pediatrician's report. Her heart rate was initially in the 80s, which was a cause for concern; the resting heart rate for an infant is usually 120 to 160 beats per minute. The report goes on:

She was dried, stimulated, positioned and suctioned, and received bag valve mask ventilation with some improvement in her heart rate and color. The patient was intubated and, due to her small size, initially it was difficult to assess the location of the endotracheal tube. She received two doses of epinephrine [adrenaline] through the endotracheal tube with minimal improvement in her heart rate, which had decreased during the intubation attempt. She also required approximately thirty seconds of chest compressions. When the patient's heart rate failed to improve, the endotracheal tube was removed and replaced with subsequent improvement of the heart rate.

The doctors suspected that the initial placement of Baby A's endotracheal tube had it in her esophagus and not her trachea, meaning it was delivering air to her stomach and not her lungs. Fortunately, the second placement worked out better. "When correct endotracheal tube position was confirmed," the report concluded, "the baby received a dose of surfactant and was then transported to the NICU for further management."

Baby Girl B, the bigger of the two at 630 grams, also appeared "blue and floppy" at birth. Her heart rate, while not as low as the 80s, was still below 100, so she, too, was bagged with oxygen and given chest compressions. The doctors had less trouble intubating Baby Girl B than they did her sister. After one attempt, her heart rate improved and she was given a dose of surfactant before being sent down to the NICU.

Reading through the reports on the delivery after the fact,

it is hard to imagine all of this happening to girls who were just 12 inches long and who weighed not much more than 1 pound apiece. The suctioning, the chest compressions, the tubes in and out and then in again—and just the mere image of all these people hovering over them and frantically trying to give them life. It was a startling welcome to the world for our daughters, especially for the little one, little Baby A.

Predictably, our babies' Apgar scores were in the low range, especially in the immediate aftermath of their birth. A system used by doctors and nurses to assess a newborn's condition, Apgars are based on a ten-point scale that accounts for everything from the baby's heart rate and color to its muscle tone and breathing; scores of 7 and above are considered normal. Both our babies started out with Apgars of just 3 at one minute, but then things started to look up. By five minutes, Baby A's Apgars were at 4 and Baby B's at 5. And by ten minutes they were at 7 and 8, respectively—a tribute to the fast work of the pediatricians in the OR. These people—all complete strangers at the time—had given our babies a chance to live. Now we could only wait and see what happened next.

Jim and I met up with Kim in the recovery room on the labor and delivery floor. It was a cramped rectangle of a room with four beds lined up in a row. Lying in the bed closest to the door, Kim was groggy and mumbling like a drunk from time to time when she opened her eyes.

In addition to the leftover effects of the general anesthesia, Kim was on generous amounts of morphine to ease the pain from the incision. She was hooked up yet again to various monitors, IVs had been reinserted into both her arms, and the catheter still was there to collect her urine, which I could see in the tube was tinged with red. Our nurse was in and out of the room every few minutes to record her vitals and to check her incision and its dressing. I couldn't bring myself to look when the nurse lifted Kim's gown.

The doctors had told us Kim would have a classic C-section: a 4-inch, up-and-down gash from the belly button south. This would allow for fast and easy access to the babies and an "atraumatic" delivery because they could easily be lifted out of Kim's belly. The more common form of C-section is a horizontal incision just below the bikini line.

The major disadvantage of the classic procedure—apart from a more prominent scar—is its impact on future deliveries. Because it is a vertical cut against the grain of the muscle, the incision from a classic C-section never heals as well as a bikini cut; the muscles are never as strong as they were before. As a result, Kim will never be able to deliver a baby vaginally; birth by cesarean is the only option.

In the recovery room, Kim stirred from time to time to mutter something about the babies or about the pain she was feeling in her belly. She kept asking if the babies were breathing. Standing at her bedside with my hand resting on top of hers, I told her they were.

"They look great," I said, exaggerating more than a little, but wanting only to ease her mind.

"Did they get their surfactant?" she mumbled, her eyes still closed.

"They got their surfactant and they're breathing," I said. I got the feeling that Kim was not really hearing me, that she wasn't really there. Her questions about the surfactant and the breathing were coming from somewhere else. She wanted to show concern and to show she understood the situation we were in, but the drugs wouldn't let her dwell on it. She had to recover first. For whatever reason, she felt that as long as the babies got their surfactant, they were doing fine. That's all she needed to know right then. It's all she wanted to know.

Kim's father left to get some lunch downstairs and I pulled a chair up alongside Kim's bed. She was sleeping. The movie *Jaws* was on the television over the recovery room door. Children were screaming as the mammoth shark attacked their boats. I turned down the sound and sat watching the pictures. The blood and the mayhem on the screen struck me as an absurd and yet a fitting backdrop to what was happening in our life.

When Kim's father returned, Kim awoke for a few minutes while Jim and I were speaking softly by her bed. She said something about cauliflower.

"What?" we asked.

"I just saw a sign made out of cauliflower," she mumbled. "The letters, they were cauliflower."

"What did they spell?" we asked.

"I don't know," she said with a smile and went back to sleep.

At about four o'clock, I told Jim I wanted to go down and check on the babies; I figured the doctors and nurses would have them stable and in their places by now. We had been in the recovery room for nearly two hours and were expecting to be back in our own room before long. Jim said he'd stay with Kim, who was still sound asleep.

Downstairs, I called into the NICU from the phone in the hall. "It's Mr. Woodwell," I said. "I'm here to see my babies."

Inside the door, I took off my watch, washed my hands and forearms at the scrub station, and put on a blue gown before venturing around the corner for the second time into C-Pod. The nurses all looked up from what they were doing and smiled. I felt their eyes on me like searchlights and imagined everyone trying to gauge my composure, everyone wondering how I'd react to seeing our babies in the NICU for the first time.

A nurse walked up to me and said she was taking care of one of the girls. She called her "Baby B" and walked me to her station. "This is the bigger one," the nurse said.

Hearing the word "bigger" applied to the infant on the warming bed before me was startling, even ridiculous. No more than a foot long, little Baby B had not an ounce of fat on her body. She looked like a skinny old woman in miniature, I thought. Her skin was bright red, like it was burned, and you could see the veins and ribs underneath.

When I had seen the babies upstairs, I hadn't known what to expect and was surprised and relieved that they were whole. Up close in the NICU and with time now to look them over from head to toe, I could see they faced an uphill climb.

Baby B was lying on her back on a flat, rectangular table about four feet above the floor; bright lights shone down on her from above to ward off jaundice. She was under a rectangular plastic hood—a see-through tent—that the nurse said would help her body retain moisture. Right now, the nurse told me, the baby's skin was of such a consistency that you could rub it off with your fingers, like the skin that forms on pudding.

The baby had on a floppy knit hat to keep her warm, but was otherwise completely naked. The hat was the only thing that looked remotely comfortable. Wires and tubes extended from her body in a tangle. She had four dime-sized monitor leads with little animal faces taped to her torso, along with a temperature sensor that was wired to the warming lamp above her bed. There was a red oximeter light wrapped around her foot, an IV tube in her umbilical cord, and another in one of her pencil-thin arms. The ventilator was held to her face with a large X of white tape that hid her cheeks and chin. Her eyes were closed.

"They're still fused shut," the nurse explained, assuring me they'd open in the next few days.

As I looked down on Baby B, I thought she looked more machine than human, like something they had created in a lab, a horrific experiment. I briefly entertained the idea that this wasn't really our baby, that we had somehow been duped. Neither of us was there to see them delivered; neither of us knew what really happened upstairs.

The nurse explained to me about all the monitors and the wires, what each was for and what it told them about how our daughter was doing. She was throwing out words like "electrolytes" and "bilirubin," and I was pretending to understand. I nodded my head and began to ask her a number of questions, but she advised me to take it slow. "There's a lot to learn," she said. "You'll have plenty of time."

The nurse then pointed me to a bed deeper in the unit to see Baby A. She said they had hoped to put our twins side by side, but there wasn't room. At our other baby's bedside, I saw all the same wires, tubes, machinery, and even a matching hat. The only difference was her size: she was noticeably smaller. Her hat fit loosely on her plum-sized head.

Our smaller baby's nurse asked if we had selected names yet. I told her we had. Over each of the girl's nursing stations were signs identifying them only as "Baby Girl A Woodwell" and "Baby Girl B Woodwell."

"Which of the babies was born first?" I asked.

Kim and I had decided that the firstborn of the twins would be Nina and the second Johanna, or Josie. We had come up with the name Johanna first and didn't want Nina to be an afterthought, both the second baby and the second name.

Standing in the NICU on the first afternoon of their lives, I wondered if I'd ever have a chance to tell our girls the story of how they got their names. Although it was obvious that their condition was tenuous and uncertain, I don't remember the nurses saying much at all that day about our babies' actual prospects. The idea, I assume, was simply to get me acquainted with the NICU and to leave it at that. Before I left, one of the nurses gave me two pictures they had taken of the babies after they were admitted.

Thursday, May 29, 2200: Seeing them in the NICU alone, I am standing in for the two of us. I don't know what to do but look at them. I lean over and talk and say "Hi baby girl," call them by their names, say they look great. The nurses tell me what's up and how they're doing, but I can't get it all straight. She's saying something about glucose levels in our baby's blood, and all I can think is, "Is this really happening? Am I really standing here in a newborn intensive care unit looking at my daughters? Are these really my daughters?" It's like I am standing in for someone else or watching as someone else goes through this. I try to ask all the right questions and look on with concern and compassion, but it's not really real yet. I wonder why I am not weeping at the sight of my own daughters, when I was ready to gush looking at others' infants the day before. It's because it's not really real.

When I returned to the eighth floor, Kim and her father were back in our room. They asked how the babies looked, and I said they looked OK. I showed Kim the pictures. She took a quick glance and handed them back to me without a word. Kim was still on an enormous amount of morphine and was still unable to grasp what was happening to us. While her father and I were talking about my visit to the NICU, Kim interrupted to say she was falling down a hill.

"Well, it's not me who's falling, it's my feet," she said. She then mumbled something about a wall in front of her bed. She said she was glad when it disappeared.

Her father then told me about the chickens. He told me Kim had been seeing purple chickens whenever she closed her eyes. Kim interrupted to say she was seeing them again. Her head was back on the pillow, her eyes were closed, and she had a big, stoned smile on her face. And she was talking about the chickens she saw. She told us they were purple, then red, then yellow. "No wait," she said. "They're cut-out cardboard chickens and they're all different colors at once."

Kim's father and I laughed. Kim found it funny too. She called the visions she saw when she closed her eyes her "screensavers." Miscellaneous objects—chickens, vegetables, whatever—running back and forth in front of her eyes, blocking her view of what was really happening to us and our little ones downstairs.

Kim soon was sound asleep again. I took the opportunity to go down the hall and call my parents and Kim's mom with an update. Kim's father and I then decided we'd go for a run. There was little else we could do, and we both were feeling a need to get outside after the day's events. We had now been in the hospital for nearly forty-eight hours, and I had only been outside once.

Kim still was sleeping when we returned, so Jim and I decided we'd take showers and go out for dinner. I felt guilty leaving Kim alone, but the nurses were checking on her every hour or so, and it seemed all she wanted to do was sleep. On our way out of the hospital, Jim and I stopped in the NICU so he could see the babies. At Nina's bedside, the nurse encouraged Jim to place his pinky in his granddaughter's tiny hand. When she grabbed hold of it with her spaghetti-like fingers, I could that see Jim was trying hard not to cry.

Nursing Progress Note. Thursday, May 29, 1900: The father of the twins has visited twice. He is tearful and is asking many very appropriate questions. He has been given a full update on what to expect during the first 48 hours of their hospitalization.

After dinner, Jim checked into a hotel near the hospital. Back in our room later that night after another brief visit with our daughters in the NICU, I tried to get some sleep.

Thursday, May 29, 2200: Kim is sleeping. The IV pumps and the monitor machines are all still going. All except the fetal monitor, which now sits dark and quiet beside the bed.

Eight

The premature baby is not merely a small baby; it is an undeveloped baby. It is not ready to be born or to live under extrauterine conditions. The younger it is, the less developed it is and the less prepared to struggle against the abnormal conditions in which it is placed. It is intended to float in warm water of a constant temperature; it has, instead, to be handled and exposed to air of all degrees of temperature. Its circulation is compelled to change from the fetal to the adult form months before it is ready for the change. It is compelled to breathe air into lungs only partially ready for use. . . . It is obliged to use digestive organs only partially completed, instead of obtaining nourishment already prepared through the circulation. In short, it is not prepared for an independent existence, and has to depend for its life on organs only partially ready to perform their functions. The more these facts are appreciated the more care and attention will be given to these infants.

—John Lovett Morse, AM, MD, Instructor in Pediatrics, Harvard Medical School, from "The Care and Feeding of Premature Infants," a paper read before the Washington Gynecological and Obstetrical Society, January 20, 1905.

As recently as ten years before they were born, around the time that Kim and I were graduating from college, Josie and Nina would have been given up for dead. Over the last four decades, the doctors and researchers working in the field of neonatology have reduced by as much as eight weeks the gestational age at which a fetus can be considered able to survive in the outside world, giving hundreds of thousands of babies a chance to live.

In the 1950s and 1960s, it was typically a death sentence to be born at or before thirty-two weeks gestation; the average gestational age of a full-term baby is forty weeks. By the 1980s, babies born between twenty-eight and thirty-one weeks had a better than 80 percent chance of survival. And today, birth at twenty-four or twenty-five weeks is no longer an automatic ticket to the morgue. Between 40 and 50 percent of these babies make it, and about an equal percentage make it without long-term disabilities.

The use of exogenous surfactant since the late 1980s is the main reason why doctors now are able to save babies born as early as twenty-four weeks. Surfactant is the lung-cell secretion that the medical student told Kim and me about during our first night in the hospital, the stuff Kim asked about again and again in the hours after the operation, wanting to make sure our babies had been given their rightful dose.

Surfactant is produced by the lung cells to coat the airways and air sacs, or alveoli. Its function is to help keep these passageways open between breaths. Production of surfactant doesn't begin, however, until twenty-four weeks gestation, and a fetus generally doesn't have a well-developed supply of it until thirty-six weeks. It is because of a lack of surfactant that the lung walls in extremely premature infants are stiff and hard. This means the baby has to expend that much more energy just to keep her lungs open. Before surfactant, many of these babies would get so tired working to breathe that they'd die trying. The alveoli eventually would collapse, cutting the flow of oxygen to the rest of the body.

The use of ventilators to help these babies breathe never solved the problem, but only introduced problems of its own. Not only are the lung walls stiff in an extremely premature infant, they are also very brittle. As a result, the constant pressure of the ventilator's mechanized breaths can easily blow holes through the baby's lungs, and it's downhill from there.

The lack of surfactant, combined with the physical immaturity of an extremely premature infant's lungs, leads to a condition called respiratory distress syndrome (RDS). Also called hyaline membrane disease (HMD), RDS is the most common respiratory problem that affects premature babies. It's what killed Patrick Bouvier Kennedy, the premature infant born to President and Mrs. John F. Kennedy in 1963. Born at nearly thirty-five weeks gestation, the child received maximum life support before succumbing to RDS and drawing an entire nation's attention to the perils of being born too soon.

Surfactant doesn't "cure" RDS, but lessens its severity, along with the risks of placing these babies on mechanical ventilators. Together with the steroids Kim had been given to help the babies' lungs develop—another very recent innovation—the surfactant gave Josie and Nina a fighting chance. As one of our doctors explained, "An infant's lungs are the last of their major organs to develop, and they need all the help they can get."

An intervention that may give these babies even more help in the future, and one that sounds like something out of science fiction, is "liquid breathing." The new procedure, which researchers recently started testing on humans, involves filling the lungs of premature infants with a mix of oxygen and a liquid called perflubron. According to researchers, the main benefit of liquid breathing is that it reduces the damage that ventilators can cause to an infant's lungs.

Liquid breathing, surfactant, and steroids, of course, are only the most recent in a long line of innovations—from incubators and new feeding techniques to mechanical ventilators and dedicated ICUs for newborns—that over the years have saved more and more premature babies' lives. The day is long past when all that could be done for a premature infant was to wrap her in wool and place her by a fire to keep her warm. Today, hundreds of millions of dollars are spent every year on the care of babies like Josie and Nina, and their decreasing rates of mortality and morbidity reflect the upsurge in investment and public attention.

According to the National Center for Health Statistics, the rate of preterm births in the United States—defined as births at less than thirty-seven completed weeks of gestation—rose 9 percent between 1990 and 1998; the increase between 1980 and 1998 was a remarkable 23 percent. One of the main reasons for the increasing incidence of prematurity is more births of twins, triplets, and "higher-order multiples," all of which are often born early.

Other causes of prematurity include cases like Kim's, where babies have to be delivered early because the pregnancy is causing health problems for the mother. Preeclampsia, preterm labor, maternal infection, separation of the placenta from the uterine wall, and abnormalities in the mother's cervix or uterus are just a few of the reasons why so many babies enter the world earlier than expected. Today, as a result of these and other causes, nearly 500,000 babies are born at a gestational age of thirty-seven weeks or less in the United States each year. These babies now account for nearly 12 percent of all births nationwide—or about one in every eight.

But a thirty-seven-week-old fetus is an entirely different creature than a fetus born at twenty-four or even thirty-two weeks. Whereas babies born at thirty-six or thirty-seven weeks often can be discharged from the hospital in a matter of days, "very preterm" infants often require weeks or months of hospitalization and are significantly more likely than their gestational elders to encounter life-threatening complications and long-term disabilities. In 1997, about 2 percent of all births in the United States were classified as very preterm—defined as birth between twenty-four and thirty-two weeks gestation.

When assessing the risks facing these babies, it is important to look at their birth weights as well as their gestational ages. Just as the number of preterm babies has shot up in recent years, the rate of babies classified as low birth weight and very low birth weight also has been on the rise. Focusing on the very low-birth-weight category—this is where Nina and Josie would be counted—the government reports that 1.42 percent of babies born in the United States in 1997 weighed less than 1500 grams, or about 3.3 pounds. This puts my daughters in the company of about 56,000 other babies born that year at birth weights that would have been unthinkable, at least in terms of the babies' survival, at the time that their parents were coming into the world.

Even today, however, these babies often face an enormous uphill fight. In 1997, very low-birth-weight babies made up 51 percent of all babies who did not survive the first year of life. Babies weighing between 1500 grams and 2499 grams, classified simply as low birth weight, accounted for an additional 14 percent of those who died before their first birthday, linking a baby's weight at birth to a remarkable two-thirds of all infant deaths.

The keepers of the nation's health statistics don't keep a separate accounting of births of extremely low-birth-weight babies—those, like Josie and Nina, who are born at less than 1000 grams, or a little more than 2 pounds. Nevertheless, a few observations can be made. As recently as the 1970s, few infants with birth weights below 750 grams (approximately 1 pound 10 ounces) were actively treated. Today, our Nina's birth weight of 500 grams (about 1 pound 2 ounces) appears to be the cutoff, but it depends. Babies as small as 12 ounces have been saved, but the smallest survivors are usually older gestationally and therefore more mature. Their problem is often that they were somehow growth restricted in the womb.

The increasing survival rates for the smallest of the small are reflected in a study of infants weighing less than 800 grams who were admitted in the 1970s, 1980s, and 1990s to the University of Washington NICU. Between 1977 and 1980, only 20 percent of the 95 infants admitted survived. But between 1986 and 1990, 49 percent of the 210 infants weighing 800 grams or less made it out of the hospital alive.

Of course, survival for the smallest and most premature infants is often not a triumph. Blindness, cerebral palsy, and long-term developmental problems are just a few of the common adverse consequences of an extremely premature birth. A 1994 study of health and developmental outcomes at early school age of 68 children with birth weights below 750 grams found them at a "serious disadvantage in every skill required for adequate performance." A 1993 study described outcomes to six months of life for infants delivered at twenty-two to twenty-five weeks and aggressively supported with intensive care. The findings: No infants survived at twenty-two weeks and virtually all survivors at twenty-three and twenty-four weeks had "significant brain abnormalities." The study's authors concluded that whether "the occasional child who is born at 23 or 24 weeks and does well justifies the considerable mortality and morbidity of the majority is a question that should be discussed by parents, health care providers, and society."

The University of Washington study suggests there has been no increase in the incidence of "major impairments" among the increasing number of infants that have been saved over the last two decades. Percentages aside, however, the fact that we are saving increasing numbers of these infants means we are subjecting more and more children and their families to complicated and often agonizing lives because of the various disabilities—many of them quite severe—that can follow in the wake of an extremely premature birth.

Today, a proportionally small number of U.S. births (approximately 7 percent) consume more than one-third of health care expenditures during the first year of life. Whether it is in society's interest to continue spending this kind of money to save some babies who would otherwise have died, and with no guarantee that they will develop into fully functioning human beings, is one of those enormously difficult questions we have created as we apply our rapidly developing technology and know-how to issues of life and death.

Nine

Friday, May 30, 0700: Kim is still asleep and I am sitting in our room thinking about our little girls downstairs and how they are struggling for life and why. And I think my daughters are showing me something. They're showing me that life is about more than going to school and getting a job and doing all those other things you're expected to do. That's not why they're struggling down there. They're struggling to live, and that means making life matter. If they can survive this struggle, their life will be their reward. And perhaps everyone they touch—including their father—will treasure his or her own life just a little bit more.

On Friday morning, I awoke, showered, talked to Kim for a bit, and then went downstairs to the hospital cafeteria for my morning paper and breakfast. I also got a cup of coffee—half decaf so I wasn't a jumble of nerves—and I brought it all back upstairs to the room. I ate my breakfast at Kim's bedside while she slept, shuffling quietly through the paper to find out what was happening in the world outside.

My wife was recovering from major surgery, and I had two very sick babies just a floor below, but I still needed my routine. I still needed to face the day.

There was nothing of any importance in the news that week, as I recall. The only story I was even remotely interested in was Bob Dylan's illness. During our first night in the hospital, I had dreamt that Bob Dylan died—this before the news even surfaced that week that he had gotten a severe respiratory infection and might not survive.

Over the years, I had become a huge fan of Dylan's music, and I wondered if my dream was my subconscious mind's way of telling me that my world was falling apart, that "everything is broken," to quote the man himself. In the middle of everything else, I could hardly give a lot of thought to Bob Dylan's health and well-being, but I still found it curious and a bit unsettling that my dream was coming true.

The Dylan news aside, the big story in the *Washington Post* that week was that the leading candidate for the chairmanship of the Joint Chiefs of Staff had had an affair while he was separated from his wife. This, apparently, was enough to disqualify him for the position, and another candidate was named. The fact that this was front-page, above-the-fold news in D.C. during a week when Kim and I were experiencing a huge, life-changing crisis reminded me how tired I had grown of the city that had been the focal point of my life and work for nearly twelve years. And it reminded me why Kim and I had moved.

Sitting in the hospital that week and scanning the *Post* when I could, I started to see Washington as even more distant, even more disconnected from real concerns and real life.

It was a city, I had always felt, that worked too hard and produced too little, a place where people were so consumed by their work—and by the "importance" of their work—that they lost sight of the fact that work is not the be-all, end-all meaning of life.

When I first arrived in Washington in the mid-1980s, it was to work as a press aide in the office of a senator from my home state of Pennsylvania. On the days that I bore the full brunt of the mind-blowing tantrums the senator regularly directed at his staff, I left the office early and just walked around outside for an hour or so like I was lost, wondering if I was indeed cut out for a life of work and bosses and the rest. I lasted eighteen months on Capitol Hill before landing a job as a press secretary for the League of Women Voters' national office. After two years there, I became an account executive in a midsized public relations firm in downtown Washington before going out on my own in 1991.

I left public relations because I never felt I was doing anything of substance. We'd get articles in the papers or get a client on the TV news or the radio, and it never seemed to matter much to anyone except the clients themselves. I realized after awhile that our clients were paying us to inflate their own egos. As long as they were in the news, then they could sleep nights knowing they mattered.

My other frustration with public relations was that there was very little actual product apart from the written work we did for our clients. Practitioners in the field, of course, will tell you that "image" or "awareness" is their product, but I was tired of trying to justify the tens of thousands of dollars we were billing people to help them achieve such sketchy ends. And I felt that by starting my own business and focusing on the writing alone, I would feel that my work had more of a purpose. I would have a product, something I could wave in front of people at the end of the day and tell them I created. Something they could actually see and hold.

I had been in business on my own for nearly six years by the time Kim was pregnant, and I had done surprisingly well. I was working out of a little home office and making more money in a year than I ever dreamed of, having graduated from college as an aimless English major with no real idea about what to do next. But I still had problems getting enthusiastic about my work. And I often wondered what the speeches and the brochures and annual reports I was writing actually accomplished or if they were even listened to or read.

Seeing the doctors and the nurses at work in the hospital that week only reinforced my feeling that my own work was essentially meaningless. Meeting the people who took care of my wife and daughters made me envious of them. They actually had a purpose. They were healing people and saving lives. And although I was certain that politics, bureaucracy, and interpersonal tensions were as much of a problem in the hospital as they are in any other working environment, I was amazed that all these people could work together with such apparent efficiency. There were doctors, residents, nurses, students, specialists, and more. All making up a team, and all of them seemingly on top of our predicament, all of them doing what they could to help. As someone who ran from organizations and all their dysfunction to work alone, I was amazed at how the system worked, and amazed that it worked at all. I could imagine all the doctors and nurses going home at night or in the morning and feeling good about what they did.

The need for a purpose—for something I could feel good about at the end of the day myself—came into even sharper focus as I watched our daughters struggle for life. It made me think there's got to be more to it, there's got to be something to struggle *for*. I wanted to be someone my daughters would be proud of, not because I was making a "respectable" income but because I was doing something different, something good. And something I felt good about.

All day Friday, Kim's only sources of comfort were ice chips and the hand-held morphine button they had given her so she could self-regulate her dosage based on how much pain she was feeling at the time. We laughed that her whole world now revolved around these two things: ice chips and morphine. When Jim or I would ask how she was feeling, she'd smile, say "That reminds me," and hit the button to let loose a numbing dose of narcotic.

Jim and I joked about setting up similar push-button contraptions for such things as ice cream and beer. Kim hit the button several times an hour.

With the morphine still coursing through her body most of the day, Kim remained only superficially there. Sitting in our room all morning, she and Jim and I had conversations about the morphine button and Kim's visions and other equally trivial things, but we never really talked about the birth or the babies downstairs. From time to time, Kim would say she hoped the girls were OK, but there wasn't real concern there. It was as if she knew she had to recover before she could begin to worry in earnest about her babies. It was as if the drugs stopped her as she was looking down from a cliff at a deep, dark ocean. They kept her from jumping in.

I began to wonder what would happen Saturday and the day after that, when Kim was slowly weaned from the drugs to face the reality of our situation.

Jim left Friday around noon. He had offered to stay through the weekend, but it didn't seem necessary. Now it was mainly a matter of waiting for Kim to recover, keeping tabs on the babies, and figuring out when to go home. Kim's mother had arranged to fly into Charlottesville from Boston on Sunday so she could be with us when we left the hospital. The doctors and nurses told us it would be a good ten days before Kim could be up and around like normal; it looked like we'd be needing all the help we could get at home.

As the doctors had promised, the HELLP syndrome symptoms started to fade shortly after the babies were born. By Friday, Kim's platelet level was again on the rise, from 57,000 at 4:00 A.M. to 69,000 at 7:45 P.M., still very low but improving. In addition to the morphine, Kim was still on the IV of magnesium sulfate as a precautionary measure in case her symptoms became worse. Our weekend nurse, Becky, was in our room every two hours to check Kim's vital signs and inspect the incision for signs of infection.

More like a camp counselor than a nurse, Becky took some of the edge off everything else that was going on. A spunky, motherly type in her 50s, she'd breeze into our room at the start of each shift to outline a plan of activities for the day. One night she even offered to take my laundry home with her and wash it; I was already starting to recycle shirts.

On Friday morning, Becky suggested we try to get Kim out of her bed and into a chair sometime during the day—just so she could sit up for a bit. Except for a couple of trips to the bathroom, Kim hadn't been up and around since Tuesday. We all talked about it as the day's big event: Kim sits in chair. Film at 11:00.

When I finally ventured to look at Kim's bare belly while

Becky was in the room to inspect the incision, I found that it didn't really bother me a whole lot. The incision looked orderly in an odd way—a series of evenly spaced staples along a straight-line cut from the belly button down. I imagined it was painful, but I didn't feel a compelling need to look away. Maybe I had been in the hospital too long by then and had seen and heard too much.

In addition to the numbing soreness from the incision, Kim was experiencing some shortness of breath throughout the day Friday. Becky had given her a hand-held device called a "coach" to blow into as a way to exercise and test her lungs. It was almost sad to watch as Kim tried to fill the chamber with enough of a breath to lift a little blue bulb into the air. We joked with Becky that if Kim could get the bulb to the top she might win a stuffed animal. But she wasn't even coming close.

Late in the day, as Kim's breathing problems continued, the doctors suspected there might be some fluid in her lungs. After a late-night dose of the diuretic Lasix, Kim seemed to be breathing better. By midnight Friday, they discontinued all of her IV fluids, including the magnesium sulfate, so she could "dry out."

Throughout the day Friday, I was going downstairs from time to time to visit the babies, just to check in. Apart from placing my pinky in their tiny hands so they could grab it, I still wasn't able to touch or hold the girls in any way. Just changing the diaper that lay flat on the warming table underneath their naked bodies—something the nurses did by lifting the babies gingerly at the knees—inevitably would cause them to desaturate because of the stress; their alarms would sound to indicate they weren't getting enough oxygen in their blood. One of the nurses showed me how to cup my hands around the babies' feet and head without touching them. She assured me they could feel the warmth of my body and were comforted.

It seemed to me that the girls were doing as well as could be expected, but the NICU nurses kept telling me we had a long road ahead of us. They also said there's usually a honeymoon period after the birth for babies this small, and that we'd have to take things one day at a time. This, we quickly learned, was the mantra of the NICU. The nurses never tell you your baby is "doing well" or even OK, just that she had "a good day." They want you to understand that you and your babies are on a roller coaster, that there will be good days and bad days, and that your babies were born extremely early and thus were disadvantaged from the start.

Like any other newborns, both Nina and Josie had lost weight in the twenty-four hours after the delivery. By noon on Friday, Nina was down to 467 grams, or just a hair over a pound. Later, we learned there was some discussion that Nina's birth weight, as measured in the delivery room, had been wrong. It was easy to see that she was remarkably smaller than her sister, smaller even than the 4-ounce difference in their birth weights would suggest.

The main problems our girls were being treated for Friday were difficulties with glucose and electrolytes, the basic body chemicals such as sodium, potassium, and calcium in the blood. The nurses assured me that Nina and Josie were merely "acting their age." It's very normal, they said, for extremely premature infants to have trouble regulating their body's basic metabolic systems. It seemed that Nina, in particular, was having a hard time keeping her electrolytes and glucose in check. She was diagnosed as hyperglycemic—too much glucose—and hyperkalemic—too much potassium—and was started on an insulin drip late Thursday night to help keep both levels down.

Nina and Josie each had been given a one-time dose of the steroid dexamethasone to increase their blood pressure. Nina also was given the drugs dopamine and Lasix to help improve her urine output. According to one of the nurses' notes, she was "voiding very small amounts." In addition, both girls were on the broad-spectrum antibiotics ampicillin and gentamicin to ward off infection. Although it sounded to me like our little girls were on an enormous assortment of drugs, the nurses said none of this was out of the ordinary for babies born as early as ours. We would just have to wait and see how their little systems kicked in.

On the plus side, both Nina and Josie had been weaned successfully to low settings on their ventilators. The combination of Kim's steroid shots and the surfactant therapy the babies had received after they were born had apparently done wonders for them. Their lungs, which everyone told me were normally the biggest problem for extremely premature babies like ours, appeared to be doing all right. The ventilator was delivering 26 percent oxygen to Nina by midday Friday, and Josie's oxygen level was set at 32 percent—both way down from the 90s shortly after the delivery on Thursday and both nearing the 21 percent oxygen content of room air. The girls' oxygen levels were regularly adjusted based on analysis of blood samples taken from their umbilical IV lines every two to three hours. If these blood gases showed the girls' lungs were doing a good job getting oxygen into their blood and getting carbon dioxide out, then the oxygen level in the ventilator would be lowered.

When the nurses asked how Kim was doing, I told them

she was OK and that we hoped to have her down to see the girls on Saturday. At least that was the plan.

Friday, May 30, 1500: In the NICU, I am still a proxy for the two of us. And I'm feeling that just like the girls get a honeymoon period after the birth, so do we. It's hard for me to deal with all of this alone. It's hard for it all to sink in when there's no one else to talk to, when Kim's still so out of it. I'll keep checking in down there for sure, but I don't think I'll become really invested until Kim and I are invested together. Of course, I care what's happening and I want to know. But I'm a little like Kim right now, I think. I can't quite dive in.

That afternoon, when the time came for Kim to sit in the chair, Becky and I stood by as she sat up and turned so her legs were dangling off the bed. She put an arm on each of our shoulders, dropped her feet to the floor, and then stood for a few seconds before pivoting to face the bed so we could lower her into the chair that I had pulled up close. Becky and I applauded this remarkable display of physical ability.

"How are you doing?" I asked.

Kim said she felt all right, a little woozy. Becky suggested that Kim stay in the chair for as long as she was comfortable, and then she left us alone. Running her hands through her hair, Kim complained that it was all matted because she'd been in bed so long. I offered to comb it. And as I pulled the comb through the tangle of knots in Kim's hair as gently as I could, I realized there was one thing—just one thing—that I would treasure coming out of this experience: I felt I had been there for her. I felt I had a purpose.

During our time in the hospital, I was Kim's lifeline to the world outside our room. I had gone out for juice or ice chips when she wanted them. I had dialed the phone so she could talk to her family and then taken the handset when she could bear to talk no more. I had helped her brush her teeth, dabbing just a little toothpaste on her toothbrush the way she likes it and then holding the bed pan to her neck while she spat. I had cleaned up after her when she vomited. And I regularly had gone out to round up a nurse when Kim was in pain, when we had a question, or when the IV pumps or the monitors sounded their unsettling alarms.

Maybe I took a secret pleasure in my role in Kim's care because she is the type that rarely wants or needs anyone else's help. The hospital provided a rare opportunity for me to show that I could be there for her—that she needed me as much as I needed her. It provided an opportunity for the two of us, both go-it-alone types, to remember that we're not two individuals but a team, and that what happens to one of us also happens to the other.

Kim sat in the chair by the bed for about an hour. After I finished combing her hair and helped her brush her teeth, we talked a bit about the babies and everything else that had happened that week. I told her what the nurses downstairs had said about approaching things one day at a time. Kim still held the morphine button tight in her hand like an unexploded grenade, but she seemed finally to be coming around to a fuller understanding of what had happened. She seemed finally to be ready to talk, ready to deal with the situation, ready to go downstairs.

After Becky and I had helped Kim back to the bed, Becky told her she'd be very tired as a result of the experience. She was right; Kim was sound asleep within minutes.

It was five o'clock at the time, and I decided to go for my now-daily run around Charlottesville and the UVA campus. It was a beautiful, late May evening, breezy and not a cloud in the sky, as I jogged around the Rotunda and down the lawn that Thomas Jefferson had designed more than two centuries before. It was summer in Charlottesville, fairly quiet. I imagined the campus bustling with students in the fall and wondered if our babies still would be there when they arrived.

For dinner that night, I went out to a Mexican restaurant near the hospital. Kim was still sleeping. Sitting at the restaurant's bar with just a magazine for company, I ate a burrito and drank a Corona with a lime in it. On the way back to the hospital, I stopped in a CD store and spent a half hour or so working slowly through the alphabet of musical offerings— rock, country, folk, whatever. Even if I end up buying nothing, it is one of my favorite ways to kill time.

Three or four CDs sparked my interest that night, including an old Bob Dylan record that was on special. I carried them with me to the front of the store. Standing in line at the register, I suddenly felt ridiculous. I had day-old, very sick twins in the hospital and a wife recovering from surgery, and I was out buying CDs. I turned around to put them back where I had found them. But then, on my way out of the store, I turned around to find them again.

On the walk back to the hospital, I wondered when I'd have a chance to listen to my new CDs. Maybe on the drives between Charlottesville and home, I thought. Life would go on.

Ten

Saturday, May 31, 0800: They took Kim off the morphine overnight. They're now giving her another pain reliever, a pill, instead. They said the morphine was slowing her down too much. I could have told them that yesterday or the day before. Anyway, you can tell she's different this morning, in a different frame of mind. She is slowly coming to realize what we're up against: the waiting, the uncertainty. We talk about how you somehow distance yourself from it for protection. Without denying it's happening, you somehow pull back just enough so you're not miserable and can actually hope for things to be OK. This will be the hardest thing we've ever done, she says. I tell her I know.

On Saturday, Kim and I were lying awake in our separate beds after an early morning visit from the night nurse. Kim asked if it would be hard going to the NICU. Her voice, I noticed, was coming back from the morphine-induced near mumble of the day before.

I said it might, but that the babies were real and breathing and their hearts were beating, and so it's hard to be depressed about it when you're there. I told her it was odd that I was more depressed in the NICU when Nina and Josie weren't there. The shock of being there the first time was obviously a part of it, but there was also the uncertainty about what would happen to us, what would happen to our babies. Now that they were there and the doctors and nurses were taking care of them, there was less to be afraid of. There was less we didn't know.

Now they were alive. Now they had a chance. I told Kim I couldn't believe they were going to all this trouble downstairs if our babies didn't have a chance. We just had to trust the doctors and nurses. We just had to believe they knew what they were doing, and that what they were doing was right.

Kim listened in silence to my predawn pep talk. I was beginning to sense she felt the babies shouldn't be anywhere but inside her. Having them on another floor of the hospital and in someone else's care was like a slap in the face. They had been taken from her before she even had a chance. She had just gotten used to having them inside her. She had just begun to enjoy feeling them grow. And now they were gone.

I imagined her thinking they couldn't survive outside her. It was just too early. They were just too small. And if they *could* survive, what did that mean? What good was she?

That morning, it occurred to me for the first time that no one had ever asked if we *wanted* our babies in the NICU. No one had ever presented this as an option or a matter of choice. They had explained to us that it would be very difficult. Even if our babies survived, they might have all sorts of problems. They told us all that. But they never followed it up with any questions about whether we wanted to subject ourselves and our babies to this.

We had to sign off on every procedure, every clinical trial that Kim and our daughters were a part of, but we never had to sign off on the biggest trial we faced. Because our society had developed the technology and the medical know-how to give these babies a chance, we had no option but to go along. Progress had forced us to this place, and I sensed that Kim wasn't sure it was a place she'd have chosen to be.

Becky's shift started at 7:00 A.M.; she appeared in our room around eight o'clock to help us start planning our day. This was supposed to be a big one. Becky and I were hoping to get Kim out of bed again so she could take a shower, and Becky had said she'd help Kim figure out how to work the breast pump so she could start expressing milk. We also thought we'd try to get Kim walking around the room or out in the hall. And, to top it all off, I was hoping I could take her downstairs in a wheelchair for the first time to see the girls.

The first order of business, after breakfast, was Kim's shower. She hadn't bathed since Tuesday and was looking forward to the feeling of being clean. After Becky and I helped her up and out of bed, she hobbled on my shoulder to the bathroom while Becky held open the bathroom door. Once there, Kim untied her hospital gown at the neck and it dropped to the floor. Her still-puffy skin was rutted all over with crisscross marks from the bed sheets.

"Never thought you'd see your wife like this," Kim said with a laugh. She pushed her hands firmly against the walls of the shower stall as we lowered her slowly to the plastic chair that she would sit on while she bathed.

"You're looking great," I said. Becky and I left her alone in the shower until she called out to say she was done. Becky changed Kim's bed sheets while we waited.

Kim looked remarkably better after the shower. Her cheeks actually had some color in them instead of the grayish white pall that had fallen over her in the aftermath of the delivery. And she seemed in better spirits, too. Becky suggested that we let her rest in bed a bit. The shower was another adventure that would surely wear her out.

Before long, one of the doctors was in the room for his morning rounds to check on Kim. I asked him if we might be able to stay in the hospital until Tuesday. Over the previous twenty-four hours, I had heard various doctors and nurses mention Sunday or Monday as possible departure dates, but I couldn't believe Kim would be up and around by then. Also, I was hoping we'd be able to spend more time with the babies before we left—especially for Kim's sake. I was desperate to see her bond with them in some way, and it was hard to know when we'd be back in Charlottesville once we were home.

The doctor said they were "up against a wall" with the insurance companies, but that he'd try to put something in Kim's chart to justify a longer stay.

Around noon, Becky and I had Kim out of bed again so she could walk around the room and in the hallway. Her steps were slow and careful, like an old man's, and she kept a hand out toward the wall so she could hold herself up in case she faltered. After several steps, she would stop and rest with one hand on the wall and the other on her sore belly. I noticed some of the other nurses watching with sympathetic smiles as Kim moved slowly through the hallway. Becky and I supplied a constant flow of encouraging words.

"Just take it easy," we told her. "You're doing great."

Back in our room again, we decided we'd get Kim ready for the trip downstairs to the NICU. She said she was up to it now. Her babies had been in the world for nearly forty-eight hours, and she had yet to see them. She was just now starting to feel conscious and aware, ready for reality—or at least as ready as she could be.

Becky left the room for a few minutes and returned with a rickety wheelchair that made the sound of a tree full of birds as it rolled bouncily along the floor; she said it was the only one she could find. We helped Kim into a second hospital gown for the trip; one was now covering her front and the other her back. After days of IVs and monitor leads extending every which way from Kim's upper body, all she had attached to her now was the urine catheter; we hung the clear, plastic container it drained into on a hook on the side of the chair.

Downstairs, I called into the NICU from outside and said it was the Woodwells. "We're here to see Josie and Nina," I said. My eyes, unexpectedly, moistened with tears at the prospect of our first visit with our daughters as a couple, our first time together as a family.

I hit the switch plate on the wall to open the NICU door and pushed Kim through, the wheelchair squealing all the way. Inside, one of the nurses rushed up to greet us. The grim expression on her face suggested all was not well.

"Nina is having some problems," she said. She said they wanted us to come in and see the girls, but that we'd have to make it a short visit. I quickly helped Kim wash and dry her hands at the scrub station inside the door and then did a hasty job on my own.

I could see that Kim already was crying as I wheeled her around the corner into C-Pod. Overnight, they had moved Josie's bed next to Nina's so our daughters were side by side; a space in the unit had opened up to make this possible. I pushed Kim through the pod to the back wall where our daughters' nurses were waiting for us by their stations. The nurses were straight-backed and a little nervous, it seemed, but both smiled graciously at the prospect of Kim's first visit with the girls. As we approached, I noticed that three doctors were conferring quietly near Nina's bed. It was clear that something was going on.

The nurses and I positioned Kim between the two stations. "Mommy's here," one of the nurses said as Kim raised herself up on the armrests of the wheelchair so she could see over the warming beds. She looked first at Josie and then at Nina; the tears had stopped before Kim began to talk for the first time to her daughters. "Hello, little girl," she said, smiling. "How are you?"

The doctors had pulled further away from Nina's bed as we approached. I noticed that two more now had joined them at the nurses' station in the center of the room. Kim was talking softly to Nina when Nina's nurse told us we'd have to go. We then said our good-byes, turned around, and left, wondering if we would ever see the littlest of our little girls again.

We weren't back in our room for five minutes before one of the doctors I had seen downstairs was up to talk to us. She explained that Nina was very sick and that they were considering various measures to try to save her. It was unclear at the time, but it seemed she was asking us how far they should go to try to keep her alive. We told her we understood that Nina was very sick and very small. We weren't expecting miracles, we said. Nothing heroic.

The same doctor was back again within minutes to say they had taken Nina off the ventilator and she had died. One of the other doctors told me later that there were clear signs early on that Nina was having more trouble than her sister adapting to the outside world and that she had started at an even greater disadvantage than anyone had given me reason to believe. Not only were the two girls remarkably different in size, but Nina's skin was "notably more thin and glossy," the doctor said. Although this was a distinction I had missed, it meant that Nina was bound to have more trouble. Even with the IVs pumping fluids into her at a steady clip, the ventilator delivering humidified air to her lungs, and the plastic tent over her body to hold off her moisture loss, she was losing more fluid than her gelatinous skin could retain.

Adding to the problem were Nina's kidneys, which showed early signs that they weren't doing their job. She still wasn't peeing much by Saturday morning, and Nina's potassium, which started in the normal range at birth, had doubled by midday Friday, meaning her kidneys weren't able to clear it from the blood. The potassium trouble was just one aspect of the "metabolic disarray" that Nina had been experiencing throughout her short life, the doctor told me, as her glucose and potassium levels remained very high despite steadily increasing doses of insulin. Her blood sugar alone, which jumped from a relatively normal level of 112 milligrams per deciliter at birth to 358 within twelve hours and a peak of 560 on Friday night, was enough to suggest serious problems. In addition, Nina's calcium level was low and her sodium level—also normal at birth—had risen steadily as her body lost more and more water.

The first sign that Nina's problems were becoming worse came when her heart rate jumped from the 140s and 150s early Saturday morning to 181 at 11:00 A.M. Soon, her nurse noticed "grossly bloody fluid" in Nina's endotracheal tube. She cleared the tube with routine suctioning and saline. Over the following hour, additional suctioning turned up "copious amounts of bright red blood," according to Nina's death report. Repeated doses of saline and epinephrine, the drug with which she had been welcomed to the world, failed to stanch the bleeding, and the doctors infused Nina with packed red blood cells in an effort to help maintain her blood volume. Soon, Nina's oxygen saturations dropped to the mid-80s and she was placed on a high-frequency ventilator, which delivers less pressure to the lungs and is considered a "rescue" therapy for infants with severe lung failure. Still no improvement. The death report concluded:

After discussions with the parents, it was decided that further interventions in Nina's care would be futile. At that time, it was decided to proceed with withdrawal of care. The patient was removed from the ventilator and ceased to have respiratory effort. She was given a small dose of fentanyl for comfort and, at 1430 hours on May 31, 1997, the infant expired.

The official cause of Nina's death was "massive pulmonary hemorrhage," or bleeding in her lungs. But at the time that she died, all that Kim and I could think was that Nina was born too soon. She didn't belong in this world.

I sat on Kim's bed after the doctor left our room. I held her and we cried. "She wasn't ready," Kim said between sobs. "She was so tiny, so fragile. She just wasn't ready."

I began to think that Kim and I weren't ready either. We were barely halfway through our first pregnancy, and now we were grieving the death of a child. It was an unfathomable turn of events—hard to believe, and even harder to accept.

Before long, Becky knocked on our door and entered with one of the NICU nurses from downstairs. They asked if we wanted to see Nina, if we wanted to hold her. Kim immediately shook her head no. Becky said she had seen Nina and that she looked very much at peace. Kim shook her head again and said she couldn't do it.

"She was so small," Kim repeated in her grief. "She wasn't ready."

The nurse returned once more an hour or so later to say they were taking Nina to the morgue. It was our last chance. Kim again said no. The nurse looked at me and I shook my head no and said thanks. I wasn't sure how I felt about seeing Nina again. I had seen her while she was alive; she had held my pinky in her hand. I would always have that, I felt. On the other hand, the nurse's insistence—the two visits to our room to ask—suggested to me that it might be a good thing, an important thing, to see her once more.

It was clear to me, however, that there was no convincing Kim. She wasn't interested, and I understood completely why. Later, another nurse brought us some of Nina's things—the hat she wore to keep her warm, the blanket from her bed, her ID bracelet, and the handwritten sign from above her station telling everyone who she was: "Woodwell, Baby A, Girl." They also gave us several sets of handprints and footprints they had made before she was taken to the morgue. The feet were no longer than the face of my wristwatch, the hands not big enough to palm a dime. Although it was hard at the time even to look at them, these are things we will always treasure. They will always remind us of the little girl we lost, the little girl who might have been.

Kim and I waited two or three hours before calling our parents with the news. With Nina we had lost the defining feature of our pregnancy: the twins. We had lost all the visions, all the dreams we had of two little girls playing together in our yard, hiding from one another in the barn, helping Kim in her garden, going off to school. Adjusting to the idea that there was only one baby now would take time. We had lost something that had become very special to us. Something we had anticipated with a kind of excitement we had never felt before. It was a once-in-a-lifetime opportunity, and now it was gone.

Sitting alone in our hospital room that afternoon, we felt defeated. We felt like giving up. We had been hit that week with such a relentless volley of bad news that we felt we no longer had the strength to defend ourselves. We could hardly think of the baby still living on the seventh floor. We now sensed it was inevitable that she, too, would be taken from us, that the whole experience would amount to nothing. We'd be back at home, alone, in the days to come. And we'd wonder why all this had happened, why we were singled out. Why?

The anger that had been building within us as the week progressed now bubbled to the top of our being. We had been so deliberate, so careful, so concerned about doing things right. I remember thinking about the woman in our parenting class back home who couldn't stop smoking. And I remember wondering how her baby was and thinking it was probably all right.

Why us? It was hard—no, impossible—to avoid the question. Horrible things were happening, and we felt we were being punished. We relentlessly searched our minds for indications that perhaps we had contributed to our own defeat. We wondered if we had become too excited about the twins, if all the talk of twins and all the buildup had become tiresome, if somehow we should have kept it quieter. We wondered if we had come to feel too special, if we had started to see the twins as a reward for something we'd done or for who we were, when they were, in fact, no more than a random act of nature.

During the course of the afternoon, Becky placed a small decal on the outside of our door to indicate we had lost a child. The stark, black-and-white image was of two silhouetted adult heads side by side and looking down on the lifeless body of a baby. Becky explained that it would help insure that none of the staff would come waltzing in to ask how our babies were doing. Nevertheless, I felt that we had been somehow marked, that the sign was like the yellow tape at a crime scene warning onlookers to keep out. "You don't want to be here," it told them. "This is a depressing place."

Becky was in and out of our room sporadically throughout the afternoon. "Patient and husband grieving over loss of daughter. Given time," she wrote on the nurse's flowsheet at one point. We cried and spoke openly about our grief while Becky was with us. We had shared so much with her already that there was nothing left to hide. Her presence in our room throughout that day was actually a comfort. We felt so horribly alone. It was good to know that someone cared, that someone was watching, keeping tabs.

Later, after a number of tearful conversations with our parents and a slow, quiet walk around the eighth floor, Kim was back in bed asleep. It was about six o'clock. Unable to sleep myself, I decided to go for a run.

Running in a wooded area by a cemetery near the UVA campus, I jogged past two identical headstones side by side under a tree. I looked at them twice, three times as I ran by.

Eleven

Later Saturday night, at around eight o'clock, we visited the NICU to check on Josie. Despite the horrible events of that day—and despite our suspicions that Josie, too, would soon be taken from us—we had to show we were there for her. Her sister, the little companion she'd grown and danced with for five months in the womb, now was gone, but Josie wasn't entirely alone. We were still there.

Kim walked with me to the elevators while I pushed the

wheelchair, which we decided we'd bring in case she got tired. Once we were in the NICU, it was hard not to notice the clean, empty bed next to Josie's. There was no trace left of our other daughter, no indication she'd been there at all. The only visible clue we'd had twins was the nametag over Josie's station, which read "Woodwell, Baby B, Girl." Baby A was already just a memory. Gone.

Kim and I stood on either side of our daughter's warming table for an update from the nurse, who told us Josie was still doing OK. No major trouble as yet, she told us, just a lot of the same commonplace problems they were trying to manage.

Kim and I listened intently to what the nurse had to say, but it was hard deep down to care right then. It was hard to escape the feeling that this was not what we wanted, not what we had planned for. We wanted twins. For five months, we were convinced we were having healthy twins. But now there was just one baby, a very sick and tiny one, on the warming table between us. All we were was angry, and it was hard to even hope.

Back upstairs and unable to sleep, we became desperate to talk to someone, anyone, about what had happened that day. Becky had offered to send for the hospital chaplain earlier in the afternoon, but we had said no. Neither of us is religious in any sense of the word—a curious fact considering that Kim's grandfather was a Methodist minister and my family had always been very active in the church. But the truth is I had never been able to bring myself to believe deep down in a higher power. And, after the events of the preceding week, it was even harder to entertain the idea that somebody up there was watching. What God would let this happen to us?

But by evening, we thought that maybe the chaplain could help us. Maybe she'd give us some new perspective on the week's events, something to think about to make us feel better. Despite our doubts, we knew deep down that there was really no reason this had happened, no cosmic explanation, nothing we had specifically done to bring it all on. And we knew it was important to talk about Nina, to be open in our grief, to cry. But knowing these things didn't help. We wondered if there were other things we should know, other ways we could cope.

The chaplain came to our room a little after nine o'clock. She introduced herself and sat at the foot of Kim's bed. I was sitting in the stool at the bedside holding Kim's hand. The lights in the room were low, as they had been all afternoon. As evening came and it grew dark outside, the room acquired a dusky, séance-like aura that set it apart from the hospital and the rest of the world. I felt like we were in a pod floating somewhere in space.

I tried to explain to the chaplain how we were feeling. I told her we felt terribly alone, that we were angry, that we didn't know whom we could trust. I told her we had a baby on the floor below and that we weren't sure we could love it with all our hearts. I told her we didn't know what to believe. We had believed so much in the pregnancy, in the idea that nothing big would go wrong, that Kim would carry our babies to term, and that we were having twins. We had believed this was something we deserved. And look where that got us. I told her we felt we had been thrown in deep water and were unable to swim. We were flailing around, looking for something to grab hold of, desperately hoping someone might throw us a line.

Kim remained silent as I spoke. The chaplain just nodded her head sympathetically. When I was done, she took a few seconds to gather her thoughts and then told us that everything we were feeling was very normal. She said this was a wound that would take time to heal. Instead of bandaging it up and hiding it from the light of day, she said it was best to keep it uncovered, to talk about it, to grieve openly. She said it appeared that Kim and I were doing all the right things—talking about it with each other, crying, letting it all out. And she said that over time we would feel better. We would never forget this, but we would feel better.

The chaplain never said one word about God or faith or religion. She never once suggested that this experience was God's will or that it had deeper meaning—both odious suggestions that we have heard from more than one person in the months since it happened. She merely affirmed what we were already thinking and gave us a green light to keep on grieving. We didn't necessarily feel better after she left, but we didn't feel like freaks either. She told us that the way we were feeling was normal and that we were dealing with our feelings in a healthy way.

What the chaplain couldn't tell us, however, was how to think about the baby downstairs. We had lost so much already. To set ourselves up and then to lose her, too, would be devastating. We didn't feel we could commit ourselves to her. We felt guilty about it, but we didn't want to go any farther out on a limb that had already let us down. Talking about it a little more in our room after the chaplain left, we decided to call down to the NICU and see if anyone there could give us answers. We still were flailing, still reaching out desperately for guidance and insight—anything anyone could tell us to help us through a long and lonely night.

It was Saturday, so the NICU social worker was not on duty; she wouldn't be back until Monday morning. I asked the woman who picked up the phone if there was anyone else we could talk to. She suggested we speak with the nurse who was taking care of Josie that night.

Tricia got on the phone and said she wasn't sure she could help us, but she'd be happy to come up to our room and talk. She said she'd get someone to cover for her and she'd be with us in a few minutes. I imagined this was an experience she was probably dreading, trying to console two parents who had just lost a baby. I imagined her thinking it was above and beyond the call of duty, something they didn't teach in nursing school.

Tricia came in and sat, like the chaplain, at the foot of Kim's bed. As I had with the chaplain, I tried to explain to her how we were feeling. I told her we wanted an idea of Josie's real chances. After losing Nina, we wanted to know how much to invest in her sister's survival. We didn't want to get our hopes up—as hard as that sounded at the time—and then have them dashed again.

Tricia once again explained that she wasn't sure she could help us. She had two daughters herself and she couldn't imagine how we felt having lost a daughter just hours before. All that she could do was to give us a better idea about Josie's condition. She couldn't tell us how Josie would do in the end—whether she would survive and, if she did, if she'd have any serious disabilities. But she could tell us how Josie was doing right then and how her situation compared with Nina's, and then leave it at that.

Tricia told us that Josie's larger size obviously counted for something, suggesting she was stronger and farther along in her development than Nina. She also said Josie was going through all the normal problems that twenty-four- and twenty-five-weekers have, and that nothing suggested to her or the doctors that Josie came into the world with any special disadvantages. Her lungs seemed to be functioning OK, she was requiring minimal ventilator support, and she had made it through the first forty-eight hours after birth, a critical period, without any major problems.

Josie was nevertheless very sick. She had come into the world a full sixteen weeks before she was due, and those sixteen weeks in the womb are critical. You can never tell exactly what problems these babies are going to have, but they are going to have problems. It is going to be a roller coaster ride from here on out, Tricia told us. There will be good days, there will be bad days, and there will be days when it will seem like it is all for naught.

"But a lot of these babies make it," Tricia concluded. "The fact that Nina died does not mean there is no hope for Josie. It just means that Nina wasn't quite ready to give it a go. With Josie, we'll just have to wait and see. It's going to be day to day for a while."

Before she left, Tricia told us we were doing the right thing in wanting to talk to someone. She said she had seen so many parents go through the NICU without knowing what to think, without asking questions, without any idea of the situation they faced. She acknowledged that it can be an enormously trying and uncertain time and that the only way to survive was to face up to it, to take it all in, and to be honest and open in your questions and how you feel.

I'm not sure Tricia's comments helped us in any real way except to confirm, like the chaplain, that what we were feeling and thinking wasn't strange. No one could have given us the answers we thought we wanted that night, because there was no real reason why this had happened to us, why Kim had to go to the hospital, why Nina had died. And there was no telling how Josie would do. It was still too early. She had a long way to go.

Lying in our separate beds early Sunday morning, Kim and I started talking about wanting to leave the hospital as soon as possible, wanting to get home. Before we had thought we wanted to stick around Charlottesville a little longer, but Nina's death changed everything. We were tired of our room, tired of all the doctors and nurses, just tired. We were hoping we'd be able to leave that afternoon once Kim's mother arrived. Physically, at least, it was apparent that Kim was in much better shape.

When one of the doctors came into our room on his morning rounds, I asked about leaving. He said we might be able to go home later in the day. I also asked if he could arrange for us to have Becky as our nurse. He said he'd check. The last thing we needed that day was a nurse we didn't know, another stranger. We had gone through so much with Becky. She was the closest thing to family in that building, the closest thing to a friend.

Becky was in our room shortly after the shift change at seven to say we would indeed be leaving in the afternoon. She said the doctors had said it was OK and that the paperwork had all been signed. Becky then presented us with a pink baby blanket she had knitted; she said she saves them for patients she bonds with, patients who go through a lot in her care. Becky said it was in memory of Nina. We all wiped tears from our eyes after Kim suggested we could wrap the little girl in it when we buried her. Becky said she'd be honored.

After breakfast, we visited the NICU to check on Josie. She was still fighting the fight, still there, which was about as much as we could have hoped for right then. When we were back in our room, Becky gave us a little talk about what to do when we got home—how to take care of Kim's incision and what Kim should and shouldn't be doing to insure a speedy recovery. Becky also asked if Kim wanted to start working with the breast pump that day, but Kim said it would be too much. She said she might try when she got home. We all knew Kim had a limited window of opportunity and should start pumping soon. But after everything else that had happened, it was too much to think about right now, too much of an investment.

When Kim's mother arrived later in the afternoon, we all wept together as we showed her the pictures of the babies and then Nina's things. Laura, clearly, was relieved to see Kim in the flesh, to see she was OK. Not 100 percent, but OK.

This was something Kim and I had taken for granted, I think, over the previous few days. Once the delivery was over and Kim was pronounced fine, the focus shifted almost entirely to the babies. Kim had gone through a life-threatening ordeal, but now that was largely forgotten. Seeing Laura with Kim—the mother relieved that her daughter was all right reminded me that in the middle of this horrible situation, we had something to be thankful for. Kim was still alive. I still had my wife.

Twelve

After a farewell visit with Josie in the NICU, we drove home with Laura in a misty rain, knowing that we'd be back in Charlottesville before long, but unsure exactly when.

The weather had turned bad while we were in the hospital, and the forecast for most of Virginia was for several days of steady showers. I told Kim and Laura that all I wanted to do was mow the grass for a few days—just sit on the mower and drive in smaller and smaller circles around the house and then the barn until everything looked well kept and nice.

I dropped Kim and Laura at the house and took off up the road in the darkening twilight to pick up the dogs. Kim had insisted she wanted them home, but I wasn't so sure. With Kim's mother in the house, I wondered if having the dogs would be too much. Driving them home—the three of them muddy, wet, and wild in the back of the car after several days away—I became even more convinced this was a bad idea. I almost turned around and took them back.

But my doubts vanished when I saw how Kim greeted the dogs at the door to our house. She had turned on the outside light and was waiting for them. Her face lit up the moment they started running at her; I hadn't seen that smile in a week. As she greeted each of the dogs—Django, Weber, and Murphy—with the high-pitched, silly banter we reserve for babies and pets, I realized that the dogs were our babies right then. They couldn't possibly mean the same thing to us as Josie and Nina, but they were something we could take care of. Better yet, they were oblivious to everything that had happened that week. It didn't matter to them that we had been in the hospital or that we had been expecting twins. They were still the dogs—needy, funny, clueless, and ours.

Over the next several evenings, I got in the habit of giving the dogs each a bath after they had spent a rainy, muddy day outside. I'd wet them with the hose, rub the shampoo deep into their fur, and then rinse them cleaner than they'd ever been before. It was the best therapy I could find in those first, very quiet days at home.

Monday, June 2: We are home now with Laura. The rain will not stop. I don't quite know what to do with myself. I'm not totally torn up and unable to function, but I'm not normal either. I'm feeling everything in short spurts of recognition about what's happened this past week—my face welling up, eyes tight. Laura bought more Kleenex at the supermarket today. She said it looked like we'd need it.

Monday was our first full day at home. While I was in my office all morning catching various people up on what had happened, Kim and Laura packed away all the baby things in the house: the twin stroller, car seats, port-a-crib, swings, baby clothes, toys, books, magazines, and more. The stuff had been everywhere. But by midday Monday, all of it was gone, hidden away in the back room on the second floor, the room we use for storage. Walking into our house that afternoon, you would have had no clue that babies or childrearing were even remotely on our minds.

Putting everything away was a fine idea with me. All the baby things only reminded us how prepared and how excited we had been about the twins. I just didn't want to lose sight of the fact that we still had a baby in the hospital, we had indeed become parents, and we still had to be there for Josie. On Monday morning at breakfast, I suggested we visit Josie on Thursday—all three of us—just to see how she was doing.

At some point, I felt, we had to start accepting the fact that she was there. We had to start reinserting ourselves, however cautiously, into her progress and her ongoing care. Kim and Laura thought this was probably a good idea, although we all decided we'd wait and see how Kim was feeling. Of course, our plans would also depend on Josie's condition. We didn't say so, but there was always the possibility that we'd need to be in Charlottesville sooner.

Things seemed to be going all right for our little girl, though. We understood that she still had a long way to go before she was out of the woods, but everything seemed relatively stable that week. There was nothing new to worry about, no major changes in her condition. Just day-to-day management and oversight of the various bodily systems— metabolism, breathing, bowels—that she hadn't had time to develop fully in the womb.

Before leaving the hospital, we arranged with the NICU to have Josie's nurse call us every night around seven o'clock. We started a journal of her progress, scribbling notes in a little, spiral-bound book as we listened to a detailed summary of our daughter's day.

Monday, June 2: OK. Good day. Down on oxygen requirements. Near room air. Starting IV nutrition.

Tuesday, June 3: Good day. Minimal settings on ventilator. Lights for bilirubin turned off. *Good.*

Wednesday, June 4: "Just fine." Minimal settings on vent; now on room air. Nothing else new. Glucose on high side, keeping an eye on it. Gave her insulin drip.

Kim was up and down our steep and narrow farmhouse stairs from the moment she got home, despite warnings from Becky and others that she take it slow. She said she basically felt fine—still a little sore, but fine. Even so, Laura handled most of the cooking that week, and I generally did the dishes. Our meals together were quiet affairs, the three of us at the big farm table in our dining room, talking from time to time about the events of the past week, wondering together what it all meant, and knowing at the same time that it meant nothing at all.

On Monday afternoon, our neighbor Clyde came by with soup; he said he couldn't believe it when he heard. His stepdaughter had been diagnosed with preeclampsia the year before and had to stay in bed for a month or more before delivering her baby. "And she's healthy just like Kim," Clyde said, clearly wondering if something strange was suddenly going on. Pregnancy is supposed to go all right. When it doesn't, it shakes your faith, your whole view of the world.

Clyde's was the first in a long line of expressions of sympathy and concern from all corners of the local community. Kim and I had only lived there two years, but the support and the comfort that came our way from our neighbors and from many of the other people we had come to know in Shenandoah County made us feel like natives, like we had been there forever. People came by with food or flowers, they sent cards, and they called to say how sorry they were to hear what happened.

Word of our misfortune apparently spread through the county like wildfire. Within days, we had heard from the real estate agent who had shown us several houses before we bought ours at auction, from the friends Kim had made working for a dried flower business in a little town just to the south, from the couple that sells us house paint, and even from the folks at the hardware store in town where we'd racked up some serious bills while we were working on the house. The church up the road sent a card. It looked like everyone in the congregation had signed it.

Our favorite card was from an older woman who lives a mile or so down our road; we knew who she was, but had never been formally introduced. "You all have been in my prayers," she wrote. "I am the person that goes up and down the road in a white station wagon."

The local folks weren't the only ones to show their concern. Former colleagues, clients, cousins, aunts, uncles, and more distant relatives all weighed in with their own expressions of sympathy and support. What was remarkable to me was how many people wrote to say that they didn't know what to say. "It is very hard to know what to say except that I am very sorry and sad." "Everything I'm contemplating writing sounds too pat." "I know there is nothing I can say, but I want you to know I am thinking of you."

It was odd to me that, in not saying much, these people were saying exactly the right thing. This wasn't a time when we needed to hear weighty pronouncements about why things happen and the meaning of life. All we needed to know was that people cared.

Kim and I were humbled by the outpouring of support. We both are basically private people; we prefer to do things on our own and without others looking on. Our move to the country, my decision to start working on my own, and Kim's pursuit of career and business opportunities in gardening all had one thing in common: They moved us away from situations where we had to deal with other people en masse, where we had to always justify what we were doing, where we had to compete. The flow of cards and phone calls and the rest gave us a new faith in people, in the innate goodness that we all carry with us through life, but that we too seldom show.

In the middle of all my other emotions, I was suddenly embarrassed at how inner-focused and how selfish I can sometimes be. And I resolved to respond as well to others' misfortunes in the future as others had responded to my own.

What we needed right then in those first days and weeks at home was for people to be doing exactly as so many of them were doing, expressing their support without passing judgment, saying they cared without telling us what to do. The best responses, we found, were those that legitimized our grief and our confusion. We were comforted most when people told us they could not possibly imagine how we were feeling, that they had no idea how hard it must be.

It is a reaction that goes against the grain of the way we approach things, the way we normally communicate, the way we normally want to jump in there, no matter the topic, and say, "I know." We are conditioned by our education to want to raise our hand and show we have an answer, to show we understand the world around us. We want to say, "I've been there. I know." But often we haven't been anywhere close and we have no idea what other people are thinking and feeling—no idea how we'd react if we were they.

Where people failed in their dealings with us, invariably, was where they tried to say or do too much. Once people found out that Nina had died, a number of them tried to compare our loss to losses they had suffered themselves. A friend of Kim's told her she understood how Kim felt because the friend had had a miscarriage. A woman I work with told me her cat had recently died, and, as a result, she could feel our pain. Of course, no one was trying deliberately to be insensitive; people just didn't know quite what to say. But in comparing their own situations to ours, they were in a sense discounting what had happened to us, putting our misfortune in a place where they could understand it when, in fact, they could never understand.

"Oh, it's not so bad" was another reaction that rubbed me wrong. More than once, it was suggested to Kim and me that we didn't really want twins, that it would have been too much work, that it's so much easier to have just one baby. Others suggested in passing that there is a reason for everything; "The Lord works in mysterious ways," they'd say.

Still others made a point of reminding us that the events that had caused our grief are not out of the ordinary, that "this happens all the time," as if the frequent occurrence of death and misfortune should make them easier to bear. In our case, it was suggested once or twice that in the not-too-distant past, childbirth was an often-precarious enterprise and couples were losing babies all the time. This, of course, was meant to make us feel better and to imply that our loss was not insurmountable, that many had survived such misfortune before. But the true effect, again, was to discount what we were feeling, to lump us in with everyone else, and to suggest that our loss had little meaning in the grand scheme of things. *It happens all the time.*

The following quote from Anne Morrow Lindbergh struck a chord. I found it in Elizabeth Mehren's *After the Darkest Hour the Sun Will Shine Again: A Parent's Guide to Coping with the Loss of a Child:*

> I resent "They lost a child too"—as though it were the same. It is never the same. Death to you is not death, not obituary notices and quiet and mourning, sermons and elegies and prayers, coffins and graves and wordy platitudes. It is not the most common experience in life—the only certainty. It is not the oldest thing we know. It is not what happened to Caesar and Dante and Milton and Mary Queen of Scots, to the soldiers in all the wars, to the sick in the plagues, to public men yesterday. It never happened before—what happened today to you. It has only happened to your little boy.

All things considered, however, we learned that perhaps the worst response of all to someone else's grief and misfortune is to say and do nothing. Several people, including close family members, told me they essentially wanted to leave Kim and me alone while we were dealing with everything. They said they didn't want to get in the way, they didn't want to bother us.

I know the feeling well. It's how I felt about my Uncle Michael, and how I justified not being in touch a whole lot after he became sick with cancer. Our inclination too often is just to shrink away and wait for things to blow over, when we could accomplish so much more by simply writing a nice note.

Grief has a way of setting people apart, of locking them up in their own little world. The important thing is for other people to enter that world from time to time and to say they care.

Thirteen

Kim and her mother and I set out on the two-hour drive to Charlottesville Thursday morning; we left the dogs in the house and expected to be back home for dinner. Kim and I were looking forward to our first visit with our daughter since we'd been home. We both knew that her prognosis was still very much up in the air, but we were heartened—as heartened as we could be, considering everything else—that she had reached her one-week birthday. A study I had found on the Internet that week said that 80 percent of premature infants surviving to day 4 were discharged from the hospital alive; those first few days are the most critical.

We had packed a bag of stuffed animals and pictures of the dogs to personalize Josie's bed and the area around it. In the NICU the week before, we had noticed that some of the babies' areas were jam-packed with animals, pictures of siblings, and toys—anything that took the institutional and technological edge off of life in the hospital and made it more like home. The nurses encouraged us to bring things. One of them had made a colorful sign with Josie's name on it for the end of her warming bed, but that was all that distinguished our baby's area. We were looking forward to making it our own, making it Josie's.

As we stepped off the elevator on the hospital's seventh floor, we were greeted by a gawky, nervous-looking intern. His caffeine eyes and wild hair suggested he'd been at the hospital for days. "You the Woodwells?" he asked abruptly. He said they'd been waiting for us. They'd been trying to reach us at home for about an hour. They had even left a message with my parents, whom we'd listed as the nearest family contact.

We asked what the problem was and, without answering, he escorted us briskly down the hall. There, outside the NICU door, was the doctor who had told us about Nina's death. I imagined that Kim and I both were thinking the same thing the moment we saw her. We were thinking Josie was dead. We were thinking we didn't have the strength to go through all this again. It was our first visit to the NICU from home, our first opportunity to reinvest ourselves in our surviving daughter's care and progress. And now, like her sister, she was in trouble. That much was clear.

"Mr. and Mrs. Woodwell, Josie has a problem," the doctor told us. "She needs surgery, and we need your consent."

She escorted us out of the main hallway and into the

NICU, where she said we could have some privacy. The doctor then disappeared without us into C-Pod and came back with a man whom she introduced as a pediatric surgeon. Together, the two explained to us that there was a perforation in Josie's bowel. That morning, Josie's nurse had noticed that our daughter's abdomen was turning bluish gray, particularly on the sides. She alerted the doctors, and a subsequent x-ray showed free air in Josie's abdominal cavity, indicating that the bowel wall had split and was spilling air and stool into the abdomen. Her belly was now notably distended and was rapidly turning a darker shade of blue.

The surgeon told us they were going to have to surgically install a drain in Josie's abdomen to get rid of all the air and stool and the other fluids that were collecting there. The goal was to cut into the abdomen and clean it out by irrigating it and then to allow the drain to "draw out the bad stuff" over a period of days. He indicated this was a very serious problem, but that the procedure had saved many babies before. As recently as two years ago, he calmly explained, he would have done major surgery on Josie to get rid of the part of the bowel that had torn. The surgery, a laparotomy, would have left an opening in Josie's abdomen to allow stool to drain from her bowel into a collecting bag, a colostomy. Her intestine would then be surgically put back together when she got bigger, probably after we had her home.

The use of the drain, however, allowed the surgeons to buy time and possibly let the bowel heal itself. If it didn't heal—a very real possibility, the surgeon told us—they would still have to do the surgery, but they could do it when she was bigger and stronger, when the chances of success were vastly greater. In the meantime, the hope was that Josie's own recovery mechanisms, combined with a vigorous regimen of antibiotics to combat the infection that would no doubt result from all this, would kick in and allow the whole episode to resolve without further intervention.

The surgeon said he needed our consent to go ahead with the surgery to place the drain. Kim by now was in tears and unable to speak; her mother softly stroked her back. I looked at Kim, shrugged my shoulders, and said something to the effect that we had no choice. Kim nodded in agreement, and the jittery intern handed me a consent form to sign. The risks of the procedure, according to the form, were "bleeding, infection, and damage to vital organs."

The surgeon, the doctor, and the intern then disappeared back into C-Pod and we were left alone in the waiting area. They had said they would find us when the surgery was complete; they all suggested we stick around for a while, even hinting that we might want to find a room in a hotel or at the Ronald McDonald House and stay overnight. The surgeon suggested it might be a day or more before we knew how the drain was working.

Looking over the barrier that blocked the view from the waiting area to C-Pod, I could see that several doctors and nurses were gathered in scrubs and masks around Josie's station. A bright lamp shined down on her warming bed from above.

After the doctors left us, I could only think of one thing: Nina's burial. We had been back and forth on the phone with my mother all week to plan it. It was scheduled for Saturday, just two days away, in a little cemetery in Pennsylvania where my parents had recently purchased a family plot. It immediately crossed my mind that we should put it off. I didn't say anything to Kim and Laura, but I worried that we might now have two babies to bury, and I thought we should do it all at once. Two burials, I suspected, would be too much to bear.

Kim and Laura and I were heading down to the cafeteria, silent and stunned, when we ran into the NICU's social worker in the hallway. She said she had heard what was happening and was very sorry. She asked if there was anything she could do. We said no thanks.

Downstairs, the three of us sat at a table in the cafeteria's outside area and ate our lunch mostly in silence. There was nothing much to say. Just when we were starting to think that maybe we'd get a break and that Josie would be OK, we had been nailed once again with bad news. It was another crippling and confidence-shaking blow. I couldn't believe this was happening; it was the stuff of horrible dreams. As someone who was generally upbeat about life—never loving it entirely, but always fairly confident that things would work themselves out—I was shaken, stunned.

Thirty-four years without a major crisis. I had lost my grandparents and a close uncle, but no one else. Fact is, I had led a relatively charmed life. I grew up in a well-to-do Pittsburgh neighborhood, the middle child of three boys, with my best friend up the street and our private boys' school just a fifteen-minute walk away. I had made my way through boarding school and college in New England without any major difficulties. And I had carved a niche for myself in Washington and was happy to discover that I had the discipline and the drive to work alone.

My deep-down confidence that the world would treat me well had always stood in contrast to my wife's hard embrace of the fact that there are no guarantees in life. It would be easy to attribute Kim's less sanguine take on life to her parents' divorce, but I suspect it's more complicated than that.

All I knew for sure as we sat outside the hospital cafeteria while our surviving daughter's life was in the hands of the surgeons was that the events of the previous week would weigh heavily on Kim for some time, serving only to reaffirm her doubts about the world and the choices she had made.

The optimistic assumptions that I had held for so long about my place in the world were shaken so by the abrupt end of our pregnancy, then by Nina's death, and now by what was happening to Josie, that I couldn't imagine how Kim was feeling, having come into this experience with a smaller reservoir of trust, a reservoir that I suspected was now completely drained.

After sitting quietly over our lunches for an hour or so, Laura, Kim, and I finally talked ourselves into returning upstairs to see how things were going. Back in the NICU, we had another conversation with Josie's surgeon, who explained that the operation was over and that we would now have to wait and see how Josie recovered. He escorted us to Josie's station, where our daughter was lying on her back with a rubber catheter as big around as a cigarette inserted into a hole in the right side of her abdomen. A clear tube extended from the catheter to a small suction bulb at the foot of Josie's warming bed. The tube was filled with a mix of yellow fluids, air and blood—the contents of our daughter's belly.

From the ribs down, Josie's midsection was an alarming shade of bluish purple, the color of a bad, bad bruise. Still on the ventilator and with all the same wires and IVs as before, she was motionless, without life. The surgeon explained that she had been given a "paralytic" to keep her from moving during the surgery. He told us it would wear off soon.

The surgeon then told us that the suction drain had been

his second choice. At first, he had installed a device designed to drain Josie's abdomen by the force of gravity, like a siphon. But soon it became clear that the initial drain wasn't working. Josie continued to bleed from both the surgery and the perforation, but nothing was coming out the drain; instead, there was a significant amount of ooze around the edges of the incision.

The surgeon told us he was pleased to see that the suction drain was drawing more. He said he generally avoids using suction on these babies because they are so small and their insides so fragile that you never know what you will suction out. It might be something important. But if suction was the only thing that was going to work for Josie, then suction it would be.

The mix of fluids and air in the suction tube was proof that the drain was working. We just didn't know how well. When we asked the doctor when he'd know if the surgery had been successful, he told us it was hard to say. After a few minutes, he left the three of us alone at Josie's bedside, unable to do much of anything but look down on our tiny and motionless daughter and hope—against all odds, it seemed—that she'd come out of this latest insult OK.

Soon, we were met at Josie's bedside by the NICU's lactation consultant, Sandra. Kim had called her the day before to say we were coming and that we'd like to see her. We had acquired a breast pump from our local hospital that week and Kim was using the machine every three or four hours, night and day, to get her milk supply going. She wanted to make sure she was doing everything right. She also wanted to find out more about how best to transport her milk to UVA from home, where we could store it there, and when Josie might start using it. Now, however, with Josie's life hanging by the thinnest of threads, it seemed like a stupid topic to talk about in much detail.

Nevertheless, we retreated with the lactation consultant to a small family room connected to the NICU. Sitting down in private with Sandra, we talked about the fact that the day's events had left us unsure whether Josie would ever have the benefit of Kim's breast milk. Sandra told us very frankly that the nurses, contrary to their usual enthusiasm about breastfeeding, had suggested that she not encourage Kim to start expressing milk. Sandra said she is sometimes branded as pushing breastfeeding on new mothers when, in fact, she often discourages it or at least stays on the fence when the baby's condition is so critical. She acknowledged that it is a major emotional investment for mothers in Kim's situation, and she said she admired Kim for wanting to do it. She then threw out the meager consolation that if Josie couldn't use Kim's milk, they could send it to a milk bank.

Sandra's comments only confirmed for me how critical Josie's situation had become. The nurses, of course, had a better idea than we did about Josie's chances, and they were telling this woman to lay off. They didn't want us to get our hopes up and then have them dashed again. They knew how hard it had been for us to lose Nina, how hard it is for any parent to lose a baby. And they knew that losing Josie would sink us lower than low. But Josie was in bad shape, and they wanted us to accept her real chances. They wanted us to be ready, or as ready as possible, to lose her and to put everything that had happened behind us.

Kim, her mother, and I talked more with Sandra about the experience of the previous week than about breastfeeding and using the pump. We all talked about how it's hard not to wonder why these things happen, how you can't blame yourself, and how it's important to talk and not keep it all inside. A very comforting presence, Sandra was as straight with us as she could be, she chose to listen more than talk, and, like everyone else who had helped us most over the previous nine days, she merely affirmed what we were feeling instead of making judgments or trying to direct our thinking.

Lactation Service Note. Thursday, June 5: Met with parents and grandmother to answer questions. Mother feels that she should pursue pumping since this is something she had always planned to do, it's the only thing she can do for the baby, and it's the only "normal" thing she can experience given the events of delivery and postpartum.

When we were through with Sandra, we returned to Josie's bedside and decided there was little more we could do in Charlottesville that day. We figured we'd go home and keep in touch with Josie's nurse that night by phone. Then Kim and I could come back Friday for another visit. In the car on the way home, we talked about the possibility of postponing Nina's burial, but Laura suggested we needed closure. Josie's troubles could go on for days or weeks. If we put off the burial, it would be like we were waiting for her to die so we could bury them together.

Kim and I agreed that no one in our family would have the stomach for a second burial. But I suppose that we and everyone around us had to accept that, with twins, we were dealing with everything times two—twice the excitement, twice the hope, and, just possibly, twice the grief.

That evening, Josie's nurse wrote an update note before she signed off for the day to sum up where things stood. This was the same nurse who had identified the problem early in the morning and who may well have saved Josie's life by acting fast to inform the doctors and get an x-ray done confirming the presence of free air. Conveniently, she had a boyfriend in radiology.

Josie was "hemodynamically unstable and critically ill," the nurse wrote that night. Her short, handwritten entry into Josie's medical records reads like a deathwatch:

> Infant's color still ashen with no spontaneous movement noted. Parents were here today and have spoken with physicians. They have returned home and can be reached by phone if necessary. . . . Continue to monitor all systems closely. Notify [physicians] of any changes and lab results as received. Keep parents informed and support as necessary.

Talking to my parents on the phone Thursday night, I told them that Josie looked very old—unmoving, pale and thin, her skin dry and peeling. I said I knew this was a result of the drugs and the lack of blood and everything else, but it made me wonder if the little girl's life was near its end. And it begged the question, "Why did she live?"

Laura and Kim and I had decided that it is self-defeating to ask "why" questions in a situation such as ours, because there were really no answers to the question about why Josie lived except that we have the technology to keep her alive, to give her a chance. And the rewards of giving her a chance were plain to see in the NICU, where a bulletin board displayed pictures of early babies, one born as small as our Nina, along with pictures of the same children smiling, playing, and laughing at one, two, or three years of age.

Thursday, June 5: I am drawn to the happy pictures of the babies who have survived the NICU. And I wonder what the parents of these babies went through, following their child's progress and ups and downs for weeks and months at a time. I try to imagine how good they must have felt when their babies came home, how in the end they had absolutely no doubt that the whole, horrible experience had been worth it. But will it be worth it for Josie? We'll have to wait and see. And if she doesn't survive, I suppose we can't be bitter, because like all those other babies, she had a chance. It's just the luck of the draw, and we should be thankful she had a chance.

Friday, June 6: Kim and I stayed up talking last night in bed. She said she was numb. I said I was too. I thought about how the morphine had numbed Kim to the surgery and the pain last week. I thought about how the surgeons had used drugs to paralyze and numb Josie. And I suddenly felt like I was on drugs, like I was paralyzed and numb just like my wife and daughter had been, unable really to connect to what's going on in our life right now.

After an initial wave of sorrow and grief—crying with Kim, breaking down on the phone as I tried to explain what was happening to my family—I now feel almost matter-of-fact, like I am watching this from some distance. I look at little Josie, all pale and hooked up to all kinds of different wires and tubes, and I know she is my daughter but it doesn't really sink in. It's like everything is happening on the surface. Is this a defense against becoming unbearably wrapped up in it? Or have I suddenly become an unfeeling person? You want to show you're upstanding and brave and all that, but then you feel guilty for not being totally devastated. It's a tug of war. No one's winning.

Kim and I set out Friday morning for Charlottesville, just as her mother and we had the day before. We had checked on Josie by telephone Thursday night and again in the morning, and there was little change in her condition. The most obvious sign of continuing problems was the fact that Josie's hematocrit, a measure of the percentage of red blood cells in her blood, remained alarmingly low, meaning her tissues and organs weren't getting the oxygen they needed. In an effort to bring up her hematocrit while promoting clotting and replacing the blood she'd lost, Josie received ten transfusions between Thursday morning and Friday at 6:00 A.M., including five units of red blood cells, two units of platelets, and three units of plasma, the liquid part of the blood. There was still no sign she was getting better, as the notes from our telephone conversations showed.

Thursday, June 5, 2100: Not much change. Still very sick but stable. BP OK. Up on ventilator rate and O_2 requirement. Big challenge: stabilize her bleeding. . . . Still getting lots of blood products. Hematocrit at 20 and dropping.

Friday, June 6, 0815: Not great. Crit still low. More blood this A.M. Requiring a lot of blood products.

Miraculously, though, once Kim and I got to the NICU around eleven o'clock, Josie seemed to be turning the corner. She was moving around in little fits of activity, and her belly was noticeably less blue. The doctors told us the drain was doing a good job pulling all the "bad stuff" out of her abdomen. The tube snaking from the hole in Josie's gut was filled with a mix of blood, fluids from inflammation, and leakage from the bowel. The doctors said they were very happy with how things were going and with the fact that they had caught Josie's problem early.

Kim and I stayed just an hour or so, still unable to do much but stand at the bedside and wait. We were back home by four o'clock that afternoon. We told Laura we wished she had come with us, considering that the only picture in her mind right then was of Josie paralyzed and blue the day before. The visit gave us new hope for our daughter. The fact that she still had a fighting chance was a needed boost as we headed to Pennsylvania to bury her sister. We still had something to hold onto, a shred of hope, as we prepared to let go of something else.

Fourteen

We buried Nina in a plot that my parents recently reserved behind the Episcopal church they attend in Ligonier, Pennsylvania, about 50 miles east of Pittsburgh. It is a beautiful spot. She is under a tree, and a brook babbles softly in the distance. Nina was the first family member to be buried there; there are six gravesites in all.

Kim, Laura, and I arrived at my parents' house on Saturday around noon. The three-hour drive from home was hard for Kim. The last time we had made the trip—just two weeks before—she was still pregnant and was doing fine. We had been looking forward to seeing my family and some of my Pittsburgh friends over the long Memorial Day weekend and were preparing for a lot of talk about the pregnancy, the twins. But now all that was gone. Driving those same roads through the mountains of West Virginia, western Maryland, and southwestern Pennsylvania only reminded us how much our lives had changed and in how short a time.

Soon after we arrived, the three of us and my parents rode in my mother's car to the funeral home in town. It was about two o'clock; the burial was at five. Kim and I had gone back and forth about whether we wanted to see Nina before she was buried; we finally decided we did. We decided we both needed another chance to say good-bye.

The five of us stood quietly around Nina's tiny casket in the center of the funeral home's expansive receiving room. Wrapped up tight in the pink blanket that our nurse, Becky, had given us, Nina looked like a little doll. Unreal.

Kim cried quietly on my shoulder while we were standing around the casket, and again in the car on the way back to my parents'. She said later that she thought it had been a mistake to see Nina. I began to wonder if seeing Nina had made Kim more doubtful about Josie's chances. Nina looked so tiny, so frail, and so lifeless that it was hard to imagine she ever breathed. And it was hard to imagine that her sister—born just 4 ounces bigger and herself near death two days before—could possibly have a fighting chance.

Back at the house, we met up with Kim's father and his wife, who had arrived while we were gone. My two brothers and their wives were there, too, along with my younger brother's eighteen-month-old son. As we passed the time before the burial, little Riley, adorable and blonde, was everywhere you looked. When we were outside enjoying the weather, he was on the lawn swinging a bat. When we were inside, he was tugging at his father's clothes or playing on his mother's lap. I remember finding it hard to be in the same room with the child for very long. The idea that Kim and I had been denied the chance to have two healthy children like Riley—and that we might still be denied the chance of having just one—was front and center in my mind whenever he was around.

Before the burial, Kim and I showed everyone a binder notebook we had filled with Nina's things: the photos of her and Josie from the first day, the blanket, the hat, the tiny footprints, and everything else the nurses had given us. We had brought the notebook because we wanted our families to view Nina as something real, we wanted them to understand our loss. No one could really know her, but they could know that she lived. And they could know that Kim and I would feel her loss for years to come. The notebook, we felt, would help them understand.

It was odd to think that all of a person's worldly possessions, all of our memories of her, could be captured in a regular-sized binder, with just five or six photo-album inserts and a pocket for the bulkier items. Most of us leave behind entire houses full of things we've collected over the years, most of it stuff we never needed. Here was a person who had left behind almost nothing. The only real mark she made was in our hearts. I remember thinking it was a nice way to go.

Thursday, June 12: Since Nina died, I have often imagined losing a child I had really come to know, an older child who had just started to develop a personality, just started to find his or her place in the world. I imagine it would be devastating. I imagine you would always wonder why, after years of love and hard work and frustration, your child had been taken away.

Losing a baby is an entirely different thing; it is a loss of something you never really had a chance to know, enjoy, or even really to care for. More than the physical loss—the loss of the person—it is the loss of an ideal. When we were talking before the burial, my older brother said Nina was the only one of us who was perfect. He was right. She never had a chance to show she was human, to reveal to us her faults. All she had was potential. She resided less on earth than in our dreams.

As we were getting dressed for the service, I called the NICU to check on Josie, hoping we'd have some good news to report to everyone, something to counter the inevitable sadness of the burial. Happily, Josie was still doing well. The nurse told me they had finally started to wean her from the high ventilator settings brought on by the surgery and the anesthesia and everything else. Josie's abdomen, according to the nurse, was now pink and "looking good." She said the doctors now were talking about removing the drain in "the next few days." The crisis, it seemed, was over. All we could do now was wait and see how Josie's bowel healed.

I opened Nina's burial service with a reading from William Wordsworth's poem, "Lucy Gray," about a little girl who is trying to make it home in a storm but never does. The parents go searching far and wide and finally find a set of small footprints. The poem concludes:

> And then an open field they crossed:
> The marks were still the same;
> They tracked them on, nor ever lost;
> And to the bridge they came.
>
> They followed from the snowy bank
> Those footmarks, one by one,
> Into the middle of the plank;
> And further there were none!
>
> —Yet some maintain that to this day
> She is a living child;
> That you may see sweet Lucy Gray
> Upon the lonesome wild.
>
> O'er rough and smooth she trips along,
> And never looks behind;
> And sings a solitary song
> That whistles in the wind.

I made it through the reading without much of a problem, although I felt myself choking up a bit at the final lines. Fact is, I made it through the whole service without much of a problem. I was finding it hard to cry anymore. I was at my own daughter's burial, and I was finding it hard to cry. I held my arm tight around Kim throughout the service as she wept softly on my shoulder.

Back at the house after the burial service, we all had dinner and then sat around in a circle in my parents' big living room and talked. Kim's father and I, with a little help from Kim, were regaling everyone with tales from the hospital about the delivery—Kim's bloody nose, the rush of doctors and nurses at our door, the morphine-induced visions Kim had of purple chickens and cauliflower words. When the group wasn't talking about what had happened in Charlottesville, we were talking about people's work, their homes, or other family members and what they were doing.

Sitting next to Kim in the living room that night with my arm around her tight, I could feel her trembling as the conversation went on. Later, in bed, she said she could hardly stand it. Here she was, so wrapped up in her grief over Nina and the experience of the previous two weeks, and all people could do was blather on like nothing had really changed. Like everything was back to normal. Like all that had happened to us was now just another story to tell.

Monday, June 9: People think they know you. They think they know how you're handling a situation. But the truth is no one knows. No one knows what happens after you leave them, when you're lying in bed or sitting over your breakfast alone and all you want to do is cry or scream. They don't know what's going on inside your head—the mind-numbing cocktail of anger and sadness and guilt. This isn't their fault. They just don't know. And so they pretend and they say you're doing great when you're really not. And this makes everybody feel better. Everybody but you.

Fifteen

Friday, June 6: Walking the dogs in the morning. They scurry across the field after some birds that take to the air as soon as the dogs approach. I wonder if we're chasing after birds ourselves, hopes that will be dashed and fly away.

"Visions of Johanna" is a hypnotic, seven-minute song on Bob Dylan's classic 1966 double album, *Blonde on Blonde*. It is a dirge-like tribute to a missing lover. Although it is unclear whether the lover is dead or just an ex, the sense of loss is palpable. The song has always been one of my standout favorites from Dylan's voluminous catalog and was part of the reason we settled on the name Johanna for one of our girls. The other part is a relative on my side of the family, an accomplished Pittsburgh painter from the early 1900s named Johanna Hailman.

After Josie was born, however, I started to wonder whether naming a child based in part on a beloved song about enormous loss and regret had been a mistake. While I often thought about the song and its lyrics during the early days of Josie's hospitalization, I couldn't bring myself to put *Blonde on Blonde* on the stereo. It was just too close. The line that kept coming to me again and again as we tried to settle into our too-quiet home between visits with our daughter was the singer's observation that it was "too concise and too clear that Johanna's not here."

The nurses warned us from the start that life in the NICU would be a roller coaster ride. During our bedside visits or our daily telephone updates, they would tell us only that our baby was having a "good day," not that she was "doing well" or that things were "looking good." They gave us no general assurances about the long term, preferring to keep us focused only on the present, only on how our baby was doing right then, and continually reminding us that she had been born very early and was "very sick."

When we asked one of the nurses what this meant—why they kept saying Josie was very sick when it was clear she was recovering from the perforation in her bowel—the nurse said Josie was born very early; her situation was still very uncertain. "This is a baby who really shouldn't be here," the nurse told us. "She'd be much better off inside Kim right now."

Kim and I were desperate to know about Josie's long-term chances or how various procedures and interventions might affect her down the line. But we soon learned to avoid these types of questions, knowing they'd be met with what we started calling a "NICU answer." The nurse or doctor would begin by telling us that "every baby is different" and then say there was really no telling how Josie might respond or how she might do. "It's still too early," they'd say. The underlying message was that Kim and I had to focus as much as we could, like the doctors and nurses, only on the here and now.

We visited Charlottesville twice during the week after Nina's burial, the first time with Kim's mother, who stayed with us through Wednesday. During our time at the hospital, there was still very little we could do at Josie's bedside. She was easily agitated by noise and touch, so we'd just cup our hands around her head and feet so she could feel our warmth.

Josie was doing best, it seemed, when she was not disturbed and could sleep and grow. The nurses were trying to leave her alone to sleep as much as possible, bundling her care in short spurts of activity: checking her vitals, pricking her foot for a blood gas, administering her medications, and turning her from front to back or vice versa so her skin would have a chance to breathe. Even this seemingly simple exercise was complicated by the fact that Josie had to be unhooked from the ventilator every time she was turned so they could reposition her head.

One of the big fears in the early days of June was that all the transfusions Josie received in the aftermath of the bowel perforation and the surgery to drain her abdomen might trigger bleeding in her brain. Known in the textbooks as an intraventricular hemorrhage, a brain bleed can be a very serious problem, with the most severe bleeds resulting in a range of health and developmental problems from cerebral palsy to hearing and vision loss.

Brain bleeds are a special threat to premature newborns because their blood vessels are immature and extremely fragile; changes in blood flow and oxygen levels can easily cause these vessels to burst. Because blood transfusions increase blood flow, they place more stress on the vessels in the brain and increase the likelihood of a bleed. In her first ten days outside her mother, Josie had at least fifteen transfusions, the majority of these in the forty-eight hours following the operation. Yet miraculously, she escaped without a bleed, according to a head ultrasound taken on June 14.

Of course, the fact that the head scan had found nothing was no guarantee that Josie wouldn't have any developmental, vision, or learning problems, just that the major cause of the most serious of these problems, a brain bleed, was not yet an issue for her. The nurses and doctors told us we were extremely lucky.

We didn't feel so lucky about the other fallout from the operation, however. The bowel perforation and the trauma of the surgery, the anesthesia, and the multiple blood transfusions had been an enormous setback for our little girl. The week before, she had been on room air on the ventilator, 21 percent oxygen. The fact that she wasn't needing extra oxygen was a remarkable sign that Josie's lungs were functioning quite well considering her very early birth. Another good sign was that Josie was taking as many as half her breaths without the assistance of the ventilator. Before her bowel burst open, there was even talk that Josie would be taken off the machine, or extubated, sometime soon. She'd be breathing on her own.

In the days after the operation, however, Josie needed a lot more help. The machine was doing almost all her breathing, and her oxygen requirement had climbed from 21 percent up into the 40s and 50s. It seemed we were back at square one. And it was only the first in a long line of setbacks that had me thinking from time to time that the roller coaster analogy for NICU life wasn't quite right. This was like being on a yo-yo, going up and down without a real purpose; a roller coaster actually moves forward.

As we got into our routine of visits in June, we found that the settings on Josie's ventilator (or the "vent," as we came to know it) were often the first thing we looked at when we approached Josie's bedside. If they were lower than before, that meant progress; she was requiring less oxygen, breathing more on her own, or both. If the settings were higher, however, we were always anxious to find out why. What had happened? Was there something wrong? It got to the point where you could gauge our mood by looking at the ventilator controls. If the settings were high, we were generally low, and vice versa.

The goal from the start was to get the settings down low enough so Josie could prove she didn't need the ventilator.

Kim and I could hardly wait. We hated the machine and were eager to see it go. The tape that held the endotracheal (ET) tube in Josie's mouth obscured most of the lower half of her face. And because the ET tube sat between Josie's vocal cords, the ventilator deprived her of her voice; we had never heard her cry. Besides, the mere fact that she had a tube in her mouth and down her throat to her lungs for so long was enormously bothersome in and of itself; sitting at her bedside I could almost feel it making my own throat sore and raw.

The worst thing about the ventilator, though, was that it was causing damage to Josie's lungs. It is one of the innumerable Catch-22s of newborn intensive care that the ventilator that gives these babies life also can compromise their health the longer they are on it. The continuous pressure of the mechanized breaths on the walls of the lungs causes scarring that can take years to heal as the lungs develop. The longer a child is on the ventilator, the more likely she is to develop bronchopulmonary dysplasia (BPD), a chronic lung disease that can cause the child to need the ventilator even longer. BPD also can mean that the child is more susceptible to viral infections and that she might have to go back to the hospital if she catches so much as a cold in those early months at home. It is far more important for the baby to be breathing in the NICU, of course, but every day on the ventilator adds to the possibility of further troubles down the road.

In addition to the vent settings, an important gauge of Josie's well-being from early on was her oxygen saturation level, or her "sats." Each of the babies in the NICU is hooked up to a pulse oximeter that monitors the amount of oxygen in the blood. The sats are measured by the little red light that wraps around the baby's hand or foot. When a baby is breathing properly and is getting enough oxygen, her sats should be in the 90s. When something's wrong, they'll usually dip, triggering the oximeter alarm to sound.

The beep-beep-beep of oximeter alarms in the NICU is like the sound of birds in the wild. In a NICU as large as UVA's, it seems someone's alarm is always going off, always making noise. It is rarely a critical situation, just something the nurses need to pay attention to. If a baby's sats stay below 90 for a prolonged period, it could mean that her oxygen or ventilator settings are too low and she's not breathing well enough on her own. Or it could mean she has other problems, such as an infection. In Josie's case, it often meant she was merely annoyed.

The oximeter alarm is the closest thing that an intubated baby has to a cry. It was because of her oximeter, in fact, that Josie gained a reputation in the NICU as a baby who would tell you when she was being bothered. Whenever anything upset her—a wet diaper, too much noise at her bedside, a new IV, or a pin prick for a blood test—she inevitably would "desat" and set off the oximeter alarm. Kim and I quickly got into the habit of hitting the alarm silence button ourselves once we knew the nurses had heard the beeping.

The nurses told us that Josie's frequent desaturations, while concerning, were a good sign; they had seen too many babies who would lie there and take it all without much response, without any protest. The nurses felt they could trust Josie to tell them when she was experiencing pain or having a problem.

The vent settings and the oximeter machine, combined with the cardiorespiratory monitor that tracked Josie's heart rate and breathing using four dime-sized monitor leads on her torso, provided a fairly complete picture of our daughter's health status at any given time. As we became increasingly familiar with these machines, we started to rely on them more and more for a sense of how our daughter was doing. In the language of the NICU, we were becoming "monitor dependent."

It is embarrassing to admit it, but sometimes when we entered the NICU I'd catch myself looking at the monitors—Josie's heart and respiratory rate, her oxygen saturations, the vent settings—before I even looked at our daughter. One doctor remarked that parents often start to see the monitors as the baby's face. Although they too seemed fixated on the monitors from time to time, particularly when Josie was very sick, the nurses encouraged us to watch for physical cues—skin color, body movements—that might offer independent signals of our child's well-being.

Josie's eyes opened for the first time on Friday, June 13. They were fused shut until then, as they would have been inside Kim. It was a thrill finally to see our daughter's little pupils darting back and forth between her eyelids. The nurses told us Josie could hardly see. But the fact that her eyes were open made her that much more of a person, that much more real.

During the week after the surgery, we were once again weaning the ventilator settings and Josie's belly had turned from blue to its former pink. She was still on antibiotics, but was requiring less medication for pain, and x-rays showed that her abdominal cavity was clear of all the bad stuff that had gathered there in the wake of the bowel perforation. The drain, it appeared, had worked.

Major surgery was still a very real possibility if Josie's bowel didn't heal quite right. The fear was that the perforation could have scarred the bowel wall enough to block things from getting through. The doctors wanted to give Josie's bowel as much time as possible to heal, so they kept her on IV feedings for most of June. They didn't want to disturb her gut.

Josie's primary food at the time was an IV substance called hyperalimentation, or "hyperal." Hyperal is a mixture of water and nutrients (proteins, fats, sugar, vitamins, and minerals) that is custom-ordered depending on an individual baby's needs. To insure that Josie was getting enough calories, the hyperal was supplemented by a creamy-white mixture of lipids. Both the hyperal and the lipids were administered continuously through IV pumps at Josie's bedside. By June 24, thanks to the IV nutrients, Josie's weight was up to 880 grams; she had almost reached the 2-pound mark.

With the pumps, the monitors, the ventilator equipment, the IVs, syringes, and everything else, Josie's station was beginning to look like a picture out of a medical supply catalogue. This was a child on an enormous amount of controlled medical support; nothing was left to chance. Every bodily function she was capable of performing was monitored and measured with extreme diligence and care. Her diapers, when wet or dirty, were weighed on the Pee Wee-brand scale at the nurses' station and their contents studied and noted on the exhaustively detailed flow sheet that tracked Josie's daily progress.

Sunday, June 15: I was at Josie's bedside this morning when the nurse took off her little diaper. It was an absolute mess. The whole BM weighed 13 grams. Her second biggest yet.

After Kim's mother left us, we got into a routine of visiting Charlottesville twice during the week and then overnight on weekends. The weekday visits were for three or four hours in the afternoon; we'd leave home at noon, be at the hospital by two, and then stay at Josie's bedside until five or six o'clock that evening. On weekends we'd stay overnight at the Ronald McDonald House, a temporary home for families with children in the hospital. Just a few blocks away, it was a clean, quiet, and convenient place to stay; and, at $15 a night, it was the best deal in town.

We rarely saw other people at the Ronald McDonald House, but one look through the "story book" in the living room downstairs convinced me it had been a wonderful resource for many families over the years. The handwritten stories by appreciative parents and siblings went into surprising detail about the often-horrific circumstances that had brought them there. There were stories of children awaiting organ transplants, children with cancer and debilitating medical conditions that mystified their doctors, and, of course, many children in the NICU.

One story I lingered over was a mother's write-up of her baby's NICU stay. The child was born with severe respiratory problems and finally went home after nine months. The mother, apparently single, had been there the entire time, staying at the Ronald McDonald House and visiting the hospital every single day.

My eyes filled with tears as I read through the story book one Saturday evening while I waited downstairs for Kim to get showered and dressed so we could go to the hospital to visit Josie. These were heroes, I felt, parents thrown into situations they could never have imagined, parents who had never asked for all that much except perhaps to have children. The pages of the book were filled with stories of courage and hope, with *life*.

I found it hard to accept that Kim and I now were in a

situation like many of these other parents. I wondered if we would be able show the same courage and the same resilience as they did.

As June dragged on, the nurses started to allow Kim and me to do more for Josie while we were at her bedside; in fact, they encouraged it. Intent on making us active, if symbolic, participants in Josie's care, they showed us how to change her doll-sized diapers, how to put lotion on her skin if it was dry, and how to hold her hands and feet in tight to her body to calm her if she was stressed. This would help her "cocoon," we were told. This was as much as we could do for Josie at the time, and there were many days when she was so agitated and so stressed that we could do nothing.

Nevertheless, it felt good to start getting involved in a more meaningful way. Thanks to the nurses, I began to feel that Kim and I were bonding with our daughter, that a connection was being made.

Sunday, June 15: Today was Father's Day, and Josie made me a card. When we arrived in the NICU, it was there above her bed. The nurses put it together, of course, but I was moved to tears when I saw it. It has a little handprint on it from Josie and says "I love you, Dad."

Kim and I quickly learned that the nurses were the only constant in the NICU, the only medical professionals we were dealing with on a day-to-day basis. Each assigned to two or three babies at a time, or just one if the baby was in bad shape, the nurses were responsible for managing their patients' often mind-boggling regimen of medications, feedings, tests and x-rays, position changes, diaper changes, baths, suction, whatever. The NICU nurse, we learned, serves as an advocate for both the babies and their parents, the first line of defense in a crisis, and a principal source of information and answers.

And, because there is no such thing as a private suite in a NICU, with parents, babies, and nurses all thrown together in one big room, it is very hard not to become attached to these people. You spend hours and entire days together, and sometimes there's not much more to do than talk. As much as they may try to resist it, the nurses—many of them young mothers themselves—develop a special fondness for the babies in their care. And the parents, who come to rely so much on the nurses for information, honesty, and an encouraging word from time to time, start to see them as friends and allies, as a lifeline.

Josie's primary nurse, Tricia, worked weekend nights. This was the same nurse who had spoken with us the night Nina died. The fact that she was our primary meant she'd take care of Josie whenever she was on duty, or as often as she could. We'd be with her Saturdays until late, sitting around Josie's bed in the high NICU chairs and talking softly about how Josie was doing, about life in the NICU, and about the latest adventures of Tricia's two daughters, who were nine and twelve at the time. Some Saturdays, we'd be there past midnight before catching the hospital shuttle to the Ronald McDonald House for some sleep.

As the month of June went on, the nurses and doctors began to discuss the need for a central line IV that would deliver fluids, nutrition, and medications directly to Josie's heart. Early on, it was often the case that Josie had three peripheral IVs going at once in her arms and legs. One was for drawing blood, and the others were for medications and the IV nutrients. The IVs were held in place with foam boards that ran the length of the leg or arm—we called these Josie's "goalie pads." Combined with the oxygen saturation monitor wrapped around a hand or a foot, this meant that all of Josie's major appendages were spoken for in some way. She might have the sat monitor on one foot and an IV on the other, and one in each of her twiglike arms. The nurses said that if she needed another IV, they would probably have to place it in her scalp.

Kim and I came to hate all the IV lines nearly as much as we hated the ventilator. We hated them for Josie's sake, knowing that the placement of an IV by a doctor or nurse can be enormously stressful for the baby. We also knew that the IVs, especially those with the foam boards attached to them, hindered Josie's movement and her use of her arms and legs to relieve stress—for example, by bringing her hands "midline" to her face or by kicking against the rolled-up blankets that the nurses surrounded her with to give her womblike boundaries.

We hated the IVs for our own sake, too. They meant that Josie's beautiful little hands and feet were hidden under armboards and gauze and tape, much like the ventilator hid her face. With so many parts of her body hidden from view, we still didn't have a real sense of our daughter as a complete person.

A central line IV is an intravenous line fed through a vein in the chest or neck into the right atrium of the heart. When I first heard about it, I couldn't imagine that they could actually do it, that they could safely stick something into our daughter's heart, which I figured was about the size of a peanut M&M. It sounded enormously risky, but the doctors assured us this was very normal and routine. A central line, they told us, is preferred over peripheral IVs because it is more permanent; it is sutured into the baby's chest. One of the nurses told us Josie was getting a central line just in time because they would soon run out of peripheral IV sites. As it was, Josie's little arms and legs were black and blue in places from the numerous IVs that had already gone bad.

The surgeons placed the central line on the afternoon of June 10. They told us the procedure went beautifully. The line went in through Josie's chest—all we could see was a big square of white tape with a tube coming out of it. With Josie's legs unencumbered by IV lines, we were free for the first time to play with her feet. I remember her little toes wrapping around my pinky, her leg pushing out against my hand. And I remember thinking she was a strong little girl.

Despite the assurances we received about the permanence of the central line, the line slipped out of Josie's heart within days; apparently, it pulled out and into an artery as Josie grew. Why the doctors hadn't suggested this was a possibility before I didn't know. In any case, it meant they'd have to do the procedure all over again. On Saturday, June 28, Josie got her second central line.

Josie had been paralyzed with a drug called Pavulon for the first central line procedure; the doctors even used arm restraints to assure she didn't move. For the second procedure, the anesthetic of choice was fentanyl. An all-purpose drug in the NICU, fentanyl is used for pain relief and, at higher doses, for sedation or anesthesia during surgery. A major side effect, however, is "respiratory depression"; fentanyl can slow down a baby's breathing. For this reason, it is used only on babies who are on ventilator support.

The second central line procedure went fine, but the side effects from the fentanyl set us way back. Josie was now requiring 100 percent oxygen, the ventilator was taking all her breaths, and the doctors ordered her feedings stopped. Once again, we were faced with a situation where our daughter was doing progressively better and then was hurled backward.

To his credit, one of the doctors told us in hindsight that they should have given Josie a diuretic prior to the surgery to clear the fluid that had accumulated in her lungs. As it was, they were giving her the diuretic after the fact, along with an asthma medication so her lungs would relax and expand. It would now be days before Josie would again be breathing on her own.

We could hardly touch her without her getting agitated, without her alarms going off. We were starting to feel we couldn't get a break.

Saturday, June 28: When we arrived in the NICU today, Josie had just gone through surgery to install the new central line. She was immobile, on her back, with the ventilator doing all her breathing and the oxygen and pressure levels set high. It's like you're back at square one sometimes. That's what's most frustrating about it. Weeks ago, it seems, she was on room air—21 percent—but today it's back at 100. You almost get mad at yourself for continuing to tell everyone everything's OK. It might sound like your daughter is putting on weight and moving right along, but she can't breathe on her own and she's not even really eating yet. That doesn't sound OK to me. Sometimes you just want to scream out and say the whole thing sucks.

Sixteen

As the month of June dragged on and Kim and I settled into a routine of shuttling back and forth between the hospital in Charlottesville and home, we entered a period when the fact that Kim had been pregnant with twins became a distant dream. It was as if we had been in a car crash and had blanked out at the moment of impact. Now awake, we had just one baby in the hospital. Our memories of the pregnancy and the delivery were tucked away somewhere deep in our minds, only to surface from time to time in short flashes of anguished recognition.

Kim had some particularly bad days. Once we were on our own, once there was no one else in the house who could monitor our moods and behavior, she would sometimes sink into a do-nothing funk. Her father's wife, after talking with friends who had lost a child, suggested to Kim that the most important thing she could do was simply to get out of bed.

"Even if you just sit in a chair all day, you've got to get up or you're done for," she said.

And so there were days in June when we weren't visiting Josie that Kim would get up, have breakfast, and then lie on the couch in the living room and watch TV. God-awful programs all day long. I'd spend the better part of these days in my office or working outside, and when I ventured into the living room to try to talk to her, she'd wave me off and ask to be left alone.

In the weeks after Nina died, a couple of people suggested that Kim and I consider counseling or group therapy—anything to help us cope with our loss. But we both felt that sitting around with other grieving parents would be weird because we were still hanging in there for our surviving daughter. I actually wondered if other parents who had lost their children might resent Kim and me for the fact that we had a child who still was alive, who still had a chance.

Nevertheless, Kim and I felt from the start that talking to someone was a good idea, that counseling in some form might help us deal with the thicket of difficult emotions we were feeling. So we called a local therapist whom a friend of Kim's had recommended, and we met with her one evening on our way home from seeing Josie in Charlottesville.

The therapist started by giving us each a piece of paper that listed a variety of psychological issues, such as anger, guilt, stress, and aloneness, and asking us to circle those that we felt applied to how we were feeling. Whereas Kim circled practically every item on the page, including all of the above, I could only bring myself to circle one: my thoughts. I explained that this was where everything was right then. I couldn't say I was totally depressed, or even necessarily sad. I was simply caught up in my thoughts. And I was finding it hard to know what to think.

After the initial trauma of watching Kim become gravely ill and then losing Nina, I was still feeling numb, still feeling unable to connect entirely to what was happening to us. When I called people whom I hadn't spoken with and started to tell them what had happened, I could hardly believe the words that were coming out of my mouth. "Emergency C-section." "Twenty-four weeks." "One of them died." It was as if someone else was talking.

I couldn't help thinking these are things that happen to other people, not me. I was determined to deal with the situation, to do what I felt was right, but at the same time I was still in a state of disbelief about what had happened. So I put it all aside and I focused instead on Josie and Kim, on my work, on the present. I was finding it hard to grieve for Nina, so I didn't even try.

Kim, more than I, felt deep in her soul the unfairness of what had happened to us. She had put her life on hold for the pregnancy, had stopped working, and had put off trying to figure out what we'd do with our farm until later. Her priorities were to get the house ready for the twins, to stay healthy, and to make sure we were prepared to take care of not one but two additions to the family. The conscientiousness with which she had approached these tasks, I am sure, made accepting what had happened that much harder to bear. Because the fact is we *were* prepared. With Kim planning to stay at home, we were prepared to take care of our twin daughters as best we could. We were so excited about it that we could hardly wait.

But now all that had changed. Now we only had one daughter, and she was not at home with Kim, but very sick and in someone else's care.

"There's not a lot for me to do right now," Kim told me one night in bed, to which I meekly replied that there might be plenty for her to do in the fall should Josie come home.

We told all of this and more to the therapist, and she assured us that everything we were feeling was very normal. The important thing, she said, was to be honest and open with each other. We told her we were trying our best, and she ended the session by telling us we didn't need her. She said it seemed to her that we were doing fine—or as fine as could be expected—and that we should call her again if we ever felt the need.

I'm not sure either of us felt a lot better after the appointment, but at least we felt we had aired things out a little. Like the chaplain and our NICU nurse on the night Nina died, the therapist had assured us that we weren't weirdos for feeling the way we felt and that our emotions were normal considering what we'd been through. She had given us an OK to carry on, which was probably all we needed at the time and all she could give.

Proof of the true psychological toll of the experience came only in my dreams. In one of the early ones, my feet were rubbing up against something at the foot of our bed. It's the place where our little dog, Murphy, usually spends the night, and I must have felt her there that night while I slept. But in the dream, I wasn't nudging our dog with my feet, I was nudging a small newborn. And it was as if I was doing this just to get a sense of the child, just to caress and touch it. Before long, a voice started telling me how to touch the child with my feet, warning me not to kick too hard at it. I realized waking up that this was the how-to voice of the NICU, where we were receiving a constant flow of advice on how to interact with and care for our child.

I had another dream later in June that my Uncle Michael was still alive, or at least I thought he was. I was at a funeral service in a cemetery—I wasn't sure if it was Michael's funeral or not—and off to the side I saw a few men helping another man who looked like Michael into a car; I could see only the top of his head. It was as if they were trying to hide the fact that he was still alive, escorting him quietly into this waiting car to drive him off while the service was still in progress. All I could think was that there was a lot in my head at the time about life and death, a lot of disbelief. I couldn't imagine that Michael and Nina were really gone, that death was so final.

As always, there were absurd dreams as well, some of them easily decipherable and others not. There were dreams about washing my hands, always washing my hands, like we were doing in the NICU. There was a dream about being back at boarding school as a freshman, trying to find my dorm room, and realizing I wouldn't last the whole semester because Josie might soon be coming home. And there was a dream about leaving the hospital with Josie. I was with my mother and Kim, and we decided to stop in a store to buy souvenirs of our time in Charlottesville. All of a sudden, three deer were running wild in the store and we followed them into a forest and were lost.

Perhaps my most disturbing dream, or the most disturbing one that I remember, came one night when Kim and I were sleeping in our guest room. This was the room we had planned to turn into the twins' nursery. And from time to time over the summer, Kim and I would sleep there because it was cooler than our own room; there was a nice breeze through the south-facing window.

In my dream, I awoke to find Kim standing up on the bed and crying in the dark. I stood on the mattress to comfort her, and she told me she hadn't been able to sleep; she couldn't stop thinking that this was the babies' room. "This is Nina's room," she said. Then, as I was holding onto Kim and she was crying on my shoulder, I noticed another person in the bed, a smaller, half-sized version of my wife. She was lying quietly under the covers where Kim had been. In an instant, with Kim's head still on my shoulder, this little person was up out of bed and holding onto my legs, her head at my waist. I realized it was Nina.

The degree to which our experience was penetrating into my subconscious was startling. In my conscious state, I was with Kim and Josie, doing work, getting chores done around the house, or reading or watching television, whatever. It seemed there was always something to do. But in my subconscious, there was clearly a process of "dealing" going on. And it was odd to think that I didn't really know what was happening in my own mind, that there was all this churning and activity there of which I was largely unaware.

Around the middle of June, I started talking to Kim about some of the things we needed to do around the house, like getting her garden going, mulching the flower beds, and painting the new living room shelves, a built-in unit that had been installed by a local cabinetmaker just a week before Kim was admitted to the hospital in May. Talk of readying the nursery was still off limits, although I was starting to suspect that we might now want to use the smaller room upstairs, my office at the time, instead of the larger guest room we had figured would work better for the twins. We had been working with a contractor to convert one of our outbuildings into a more permanent office for me, and I figured I'd be out of the smaller room by fall.

I started talking about things we needed to do because I felt it was time to try to restore a little normalcy to our life at home. Despite the fact that she was still not supposed to exercise or do real work around the house, I was desperate to see Kim up and around and doing the things she liked to do. I knew she needed time to heal and grieve the end of the pregnancy and the loss of Nina, but I couldn't accept that doing next to nothing was good for her or would help her cope.

If there was any tension between Kim and me during the early days of Josie's hospitalization, this was the cause of it. Although I was still trying to pin down my feelings about everything that had happened to us, I was starting to feel that I was moving on in a way. And I was slowly but surely becoming hopeful about Josie's chances. I was starting to embrace the idea that she might live.

Kim, on the other hand, was still in an entirely different place. She wasn't ready yet to put anything that had happened behind her, and she still couldn't get over the feeling that we had gotten a raw deal, that we didn't deserve this. I suspected she felt she had gambled and lost. And the last thing she wanted to do was to gamble again, to get her hopes up about Josie when Josie's chances were still unsure. Anytime I mentioned the possibility that Josie might make it, Kim reminded me it was just that—a possibility—and that we wouldn't know for awhile how our surviving daughter would do.

Sunday, June 15: My mother comes later today. We'll go to Charlottesville with her tomorrow. After that, it looks like we'll be alone for a bit—the first time since this all happened, really. I'm not scared, just a little concerned about what Kim will do when I'm here in my office or doing something else. The problem is she's not really supposed to do much. She's still healing, I suppose, in all kinds of ways.

Despite her grief and the torrent of other emotions she was feeling, Kim began to emerge from her shell as we entered the second half of June. From time to time, I'd see her out weeding, edging her flowerbeds, or walking on the road. She was approaching life tentatively, slowly, like it was a dog that might bite. It was clear she had very little interest in doing too much too fast.

The one sign that Kim was still in the fight for Josie, that she hadn't given up, was the fact that she was still pumping. Four or five times a day for as long as a half hour each, she'd attach that horrible machine to her breasts and express milk in the hope that our daughter would someday be able to use it. The stand-up freezer Kim had bought the year before for storing vegetables and meat was slowly filling up with little, dated bags of frozen breast milk.

Seventeen

From time to time during our NICU visits, I'd look over at the area immediately adjacent to the C-Pod unit where Josie and the other extremely low-birth-weight babies were cared for. Called D-Pod, it's where they start getting babies and families ready to go home. C-Pod babies "graduate" to D-Pod when they get big and when they no longer need intensive, hour-to-hour care.

Weekends were an especially busy time in D-Pod. Some of the families lived far away, and Saturday or Sunday was the only time they could all get together in Charlottesville. Watching them from our little station in C-Pod, where we still couldn't even hold our daughter off her bed, it was like seeing a vision of where we hoped we'd be in a few months. It was like a dream, really—mothers rocking back and forth with their babies in their arms, fathers smiling and holding their newborns a little awkwardly at arm's length and making faces, siblings peering over the top of a new brother or sister's crib, and everyone taking pictures. It was a happy place, it seemed to me, as happy as a place called "D-Pod" could be. And I realized there was a whole different dynamic at work in our little space: uncertainty.

When the doctors placed Josie's initial central line IV on June 10, they said it was because she would be there awhile. The central line, they told us, would offer a reliable, long-term means of administering Josie's IV medications and feedings. It was the first time anyone had indicated to us that this wasn't a short-term venture, that Josie had a future.

By the end of the month, the nurses were inserting phrases such as "when she goes home" or "until she goes home" into their conversations with us. "She may still be on the aminophylline when she goes home," one of them would say. Another might observe, "You'll get CPR training before she goes home." Little did they know how much we latched onto their words, how much we were heartened by their confidence that Josie would indeed be coming home.

Josie didn't weigh much more than 2 pounds and she still wasn't even using her stomach to eat, but we were finally getting a sense that there was light at the end of the long, dark tunnel we had entered in May. Although we were reminded practically every day of problems we could still run into—an infection, vision and hearing loss, developmental problems, and more—we started to feel that the life-and-death struggle was over. We started to grab hold of the possibility of a happy ending. By the end of June, we were talking seriously about wanting to be in Charlottesville more and wanting to play a more active part in Josie's care.

Thursday, June 12: Today, I am feeling for the first time that we're in this for the long haul. The things I am hearing, the way the doctors and nurses are talking, and the way Josie is looking, it's hard not to be optimistic. Yes, I know there could be tough times ahead, but I am very hopeful. I'm not certain Kim shares this view. Every time we start talking long-term, she adds a little "we hope" or "if we get there." It's a defense mechanism and a very natural one. She lost Nina and still wants to be prepared to lose Josie. She won't yet abide talk about what we do in July and whether we want to be in Charlottesville more. Let's get through the next couple of weeks, she says.

Tuesday, June 17: I think we're feeling more and more drawn to Charlottesville, more and more bonded with our little girl. As we have said many times, it is hard in a way to grieve for Nina right now. All that has been put aside as we get involved in Josie's fight for life. There is not a lot to do at Josie's bedside, but you just want to be there, if only for an hour or two. The other night, Josie's oximeter alarm went off just as we were leaving the NICU. It wasn't a big deal, but the nurse said Josie knew we were going. It makes you wonder.

Wednesday, June 25: This week, I think we're sensing more and more that Josie has a very good chance of making it. It is not a question we have ever asked directly of our nurses or doctors, probably because we feared a negative answer and probably because the scare with the bowel perforation the other week had everyone waiting to see how she recovered. Anyway, the more we see her and the more we talk to the nurses, the more we get a sense that this is for real. This is not a huge science experiment concocted to find out how long she can make it. It is a 100 percent for-real, life-saving venture.

In the several days following the surgery to place Josie's second central line IV, the doctors and nurses slowly but surely were able to wean her from the high ventilator and oxygen settings made necessary by the respiratory depression Josie suffered in the aftermath of the operation. By July 3, the ventilator was set at 26 breaths per minute, meaning Josie was once again doing about half her breathing on her own. Her oxygen requirement was down from 100 percent, but was still on the high side because Josie was having frequent desaturations when the oxygen content of her blood would drop, triggering the beep-beep-beep of her oximeter alarm. We were getting a sense that it would still be a while before Josie could be taken off the ventilator, before she could breathe entirely on her own and without any mechanical support.

One of the major challenges now was managing Josie's apnea and bradycardia spells. Referred to in the NICU as "As and Bs," they are a one-two punch that normally starts when the baby becomes apneic, or temporarily stops breathing. The lack of oxygen then causes the baby's heart rate to drop precipitously. This is bradycardia. Being on the ventilator doesn't mean a baby can't have As and Bs. At times, the ventilator was relying on Josie to do half the breathing on her own. When she didn't do her part, her heart rate usually would drop.

Watching an A-and-B episode can be extremely difficult for a parent. There's usually no sign it's happening until you hear the monitor alarm sound, and then you look up at the screen and you see that your baby's heart rate has tanked to the 50s, 60s, or 70s from its usual rate of 140 or more. Looking back at your child, you start to notice that her skin color is changing, especially around the eyes and mouth, from a healthy pink to a dusky blue.

Apnea and bradycardia are very common problems in the NICU; they can be very serious problems, too. The fear is that the baby isn't getting enough blood and oxygen to her brain and organs. The longer an episode, the greater the fear.

Apnea alone affects one in four premature babies and more

than four in five babies born at less than 2½ pounds. Called "apnea of prematurity" to distinguish it from the types of apnea that can affect adults, such as sleep apnea, it is most often related to the immaturity of the brain and central nervous system; for fifteen or twenty seconds, the babies simply forget to breathe.

Often, babies will pull themselves out of an A-and-B spell when they resume breathing after a few seconds. But it's not at all uncommon for a nurse to have to intervene, usually by stimulating the baby in some way to wake up the central nervous system and get her breathing again. Rubbing the baby's back or the soles of her feet is often all it takes. The worst episodes respond only to "bagging," a scenario in which the nurse holds an oxygen mask over the baby's nose and mouth and hand pumps additional breaths into the lungs by squeezing a rubber pouch. When the baby is on a ventilator, the nurse has to disconnect it at the baby's mouth and hook up the oxygen bag in its place—all while the parents stand by frightened and silent, hoping everything will be all right.

Tuesday, July 22: Another dream last night about Josie. I was standing far, far away from her bed—across a field, it seemed. We were outside. There were no nurses around and her heart rate started to drop. I squinted to see the number on the monitor: 100, down to 80, and then 60 and 40. I tried to run to get to her but it was so far away. It was taking too long and I wasn't really getting anywhere, I wasn't making any progress. I watched from afar as her heart rate remained stuck in the 40s—helpless and fearful, convinced this was a major problem.

Josie was more susceptible than most babies to having As and Bs; she was averaging around ten spells a day during late June and early July. Hospitals keep close track of As and Bs because they can tell a lot about a baby's development and growth; both apnea and bradycardia disappear as the infant's central nervous system matures. Another reason to keep track of them is that an inordinate amount of spells over a short period of time can mean the baby is having other problems, such as an infection.

The majority of Josie's As and Bs were resolved by self-stimulation, meaning Josie's system caught itself after a few seconds and her heart rate and breathing resumed at a normal rate on their own. Still, Josie did a fine job keeping the nurses on their toes. She'd have people running to her station several times a day to stimulate her out of an A and B or, in the worst cases, to reach for the oxygen bag and pump her full of assisted breaths. Before long, Kim and I became quite good at responding to As and Bs ourselves, tickling the bottom of Josie's feet or giving the girl a little shake to bring her back once the alarms had sounded.

Starting in mid-June, the doctors had Josie on a drug called aminophylline, a central nervous system stimulant, to try to control the As and Bs. The doctors also prescribed caffeine to treat the problem. Neither of the drugs seemed to do much for Josie, though. We often joked with the nurses that they should simply start an IV drip of one of the espresso drinks we all stood in line for in the hospital cafeteria to get Josie's system working right.

The As and Bs aside, the focus in the early days of July was on Josie's feeding. By the end of June, she had joined the "Kilo Club," weighing in at roughly 1000 grams, or just over 2 pounds. It was strange to see our daughter gaining weight without really eating in the traditional sense. She was still just on IV fluids—the hyperal concoction of water and nutrients along with the IV of straight lipids.

Josie was nearly a month old before they first tried to feed her via a tube through her mouth to her stomach, a technique conceived to deal with the fact that premature babies aren't able to suck or coordinate their breathing and eating until a gestational age of thirty-two weeks at the earliest. Before they could go ahead with the tube feeding, the doctors used x-rays to follow a small amount of barium dye through Josie's gut. The idea was to make sure that there was a clear path, that the bowel hadn't scarred and blocked up in some way as a result of the perforation.

Thursday, June 19: Went to Charlottesville today and Josie seems to be doing fine, although they are subjecting her to innumerable x-rays, it seems, to trace the course of the dye through her bowels. This after we left the other day to a chorus of "the best thing we can do now is to leave her alone and let her grow." You can't help but feel she's being messed with too much. And all those damn x-rays. They ask us to stand 12 feet away while they do them. If they're worried about us, you have to wonder about the impact of all that radiation on a little 2-pound girl.

Josie passed the barium test to everyone's relief. The doctors, in particular, were amazed that her bowel had healed so well and without a hitch. They told us there was still a remote possibility of surgery if she had feeding problems, but that everything looked all right.

The doctors wasted no time initiating Josie's tube feedings. It gave me the creeps to think about it, but Josie now had two tubes down her throat, the ventilator's ET tube in her trachea and the feeding tube in her esophagus to her stomach. The feeding tube went in the day after the barium test came out positive, and they used it to start Josie on ridiculously meager amounts of pedialite, a crystal clear liquid packed with nutrients but more benign on the digestive system than breast milk or formula. The initial feedings totaled less than 1 cc, or about 1/30 ounce. The idea was to jump-start Josie's digestive system, which hadn't yet been asked to process anything but the barium dye.

Josie was still on the IV nutrients to keep her nourished and to keep the calories pumping into her while they experimented with ever-increasing amounts of pedialite. They would feed her and then a few hours later suction out the contents of her stomach with a syringe. This allowed them to see whether she was digesting her food or whether it was still sitting there, unconsumed, inside her. Early on, I found I could hardly watch as the nurse extracted the contents of my daughter's stomach into a 10-cc syringe. As with everything else, however, the procedure quickly became routine, and I watched without so much as a flinch.

The first few times they fed Josie via the tube, it didn't seem that the food was moving through her system. There was too much still in her stomach; the nurses called this leftover amount "aspirate" or "residual." After more x-rays, they found nothing suggesting there was a problem, and they started the feedings again. This time the residuals weren't nearly as abundant as before. Josie's digestive system, it seemed, was finally kicking in.

Once the doctors were confident that Josie was handling the pedialite without a problem, they began to mix Kim's breast milk into the feedings. Again, this was a very slow and deliberate process, with the initial feedings consisting of three parts pedialite to one part breast milk. The total feeding amount was still insignificant and small; Josie was still getting the bulk of her nourishment and calories from IV fluids.

The goal was still to test her system, to make sure Josie could handle ever-increasing amounts, together with increasing concentrations of breast milk. At first, the feedings were scheduled for every hour; they soon moved to every two. Prior to each feeding, the nurses would check what was left in Josie's stomach from the feeding before. If there was nothing left or very little, then it meant she was doing all right.

By July 4, Josie was up to half-strength breast milk. A day later, she was up to full strength. The feeding amounts then increased slowly but surely. By July 11, she was getting 10¼ cc of full-strength breast milk, or about ⅓ ounce.

After the bowel perforation the month before, the doctors and nurses—and we, too—were amazed that Josie was doing such a good job tolerating her feedings. And I am sure Kim felt comforted to have her daughter finally benefiting from Mom's milk. All the pumping Kim was doing was finally starting to pay off for our little girl.

Josie was still on the ventilator, but the progress with the feedings made us start to feel we were getting somewhere. We started to believe that a child could actually make progress in the NICU, that every step ahead wasn't followed shortly by another step back.

Sensing that Josie was starting down the road to home— that she would in all likelihood survive this ordeal—we began to worry about other things. All of a sudden at the start of July, we found ourselves preoccupied with concerns about how the NICU environment and Josie's day-to-day care were affecting her development and growth.

It sounds strange, but I think I was more stressed about

Josie at the start of July than I was during those early weeks, when her life was essentially in the balance. In July, I started to see it as a struggle not just for life, but for a normal life. Anything that could impact her development—bright lights, loud noises, too much stimulation, inconsistent nursing—now became a concern. Whereas before it was life or death and Kim and I and the nurses could do very little to force the issue—it was essentially in the doctor's hands—in July I started to see the nurses and the daily life in the NICU as more and more important in determining the quality of the life that our daughter would lead.

The level of noise in the NICU had been a concern from the start. All too often, we would see doctors and nurses talking loudly over Josie's bed when it was clear this disturbed her. To be honest, we'd often catch ourselves doing the same thing from time to time, but we soon learned to keep it down and to tell others to do the same.

The NICU's fluorescent lights were another worry; I had read a couple of articles linking the bright lights in many NICUs to blindness and other problems. As a result, we often encouraged the nurses to turn off the lights above Josie's bed whenever they could. Most of them already were sensitive to this stuff, but it's easy to forget. We also got in the habit of closing the blinds in the window near Josie's station to keep out the bright afternoon sun.

More concerning than anything else at the time, however, was the consistency of Josie's nursing care. The fact that her primary nurse worked weekends put us at a bit of a disadvantage during the week. Toward the end of June, we started to notice that Josie was being taken care of by a different nurse practically every time we visited or called—this in a place that tries to emphasize "consistency of care." Part of the problem was that one of the nurses who regularly took care of Josie during the week was having knee surgery and another was on a five-week sabbatical.

While we had grown extremely close with several of the nurses who were taking care of Josie, others were complete strangers. Our concern was that they didn't *know* our daughter, didn't understand her likes and dislikes—for example, how she liked to sleep on her belly and not her back, how she hated noise and too much talking, and how she loved to listen to the tape I had made her of quiet folk and country songs on the portable cassette player we left by her bed.

It was easy to understand how having the same nurses time and again would be a good thing for a NICU baby. For twenty-four hours a day, every day, these nurses are the child's parents, babysitters, and primary caregivers all in one. They feed and bathe the child and administer her medications. They try to comfort her when she is unhappy or stressed. They make the child's bed, rolling up blankets and placing them just so to provide comforting, womblike boundaries. And they continuously monitor the child's vital signs and behavior for hints of a problem.

Creating a system where nurses can develop a familiarity with each child's personality, quirks, and special needs is obviously important. Kim and I quickly learned, however, that this is easier said than done, especially in a large NICU like UVA's with its seventy or so nurses and all their different shifts. Nevertheless, within days after we first approached one of the senior nurses about the consistency of Josie's care, we had a "primary team" assigned to our daughter and were assured that the same nurses would take care of her as much as possible.

Monday, July 7: I feel we're entering a new phase in all this. It's very positive, really—the parents starting to become more knowledgeable, more comfortable with the procedures in the NICU, comfortable enough to start questioning how certain things are being handled. But it's also a little unnerving because it's a realization once and for all that your baby's fate is in the hands of others, that their decisions, not yours, will determine how she does. To the extent that we can be involved in those decisions, great. But the truth is we're only there a fraction of the time.

Kim's and my concerns about Josie's developmental progress were relieved somewhat by a specialist on the UVA staff who sat at our daughter's bedside for an hour one afternoon late in June to study her behavior. The purpose of her observation was to gauge how Josie was doing developmentally and to provide insights to the nurses on how best to take care of our little girl.

In addition to suggesting that Josie was doing fine, the specialist's report provides a good, patient's-eye view of what goes on in the course of a normal day in the NICU—the steady buzz of activity and the unending struggle by the little ones to cope.

Behavioral Observation. June 26: 1. Environment at large: Josie was bedded on a warming table, which was positioned against the back wall of C-Pod. Her bedspace was near a window. The overhead lighting was off in the pod with the exception of the lights over the workspace. There were four caregivers in the pod as the observation began. The sounds of monitors alarming was noted along with quiet discussion.

2. Bedspace and bedding: Josie was positioned on a colorful blanket from home with rolls on either side of her underneath the blanket. She was swaddled with a folded cloth diaper at her shoulders and another at her hips. Pictures and toys from home were hanging above her bed and laying at the foot of the bed.

3. Behavioral baseline: As the observation began, Josie was positioned on her right side with her head in a midline position. Her hands were flexed and her legs extended. Her skin color was pink and her oximeter reading was 100 with a respiratory rate of 59 [breaths per minute] as counted by direct observation. The respiratory therapist had just finished adjusting her endotracheal tubing, which was taped to her face with a stabilizer. Josie appeared to be drowsy but still restless and awake. Her leg stretching and bending continued and she also tucked her trunk bringing her knees up closer to her stomach.

Three minutes into the observation the overhead lights were turned on. At this point Josie began to suck vigorously on her ET tube, she splayed her fingers and then brought her hand up to her face while pushing her feet into the bedding. Her saturations as measured by the oximeter dropped to 91, then 80. Josie's bedside nurse adjusted her bedding and removed and replaced the open disposable diaper underneath. Her saturations rose to 97 and 100 over the next four minutes. Josie smiled twice and brought her hand up to grasp her ET tube.

Josie ceased the stretching movements of her arms and legs and then settled in a flexed position with a flexed trunk with one hand on her face and the other grasping her ET tube. Her eyes were moving under her closed eyelids and then she opened her eyes for a period of nearly four minutes. Her respiratory rate was variable with many sighs, but no pauses were noted. She appeared to be in a light sleep state with her eyes closed but continued stretching movements of her arms and legs and some generalized squirming. The sound of a monitor in a neighboring bedspace was heard and then silenced. Josie smiled again and then began sucking rhythmically on her ET tube. Her oximeter reading was in the 90 to 100 range for over 10 minutes. The neighboring monitor continued alarming intermittently and her color paled momentarily, but her oximeter continued to read in the high 90s. She maintained her hand on her face. Josie frowned and then smiled as the intercom came on for a few seconds and then went off.

4. Behavior during caregiving: Josie's bedside nurse approached the warming table about 32 minutes after the observation began.

Josie's stretching movements had increased with several twitches noted, just prior to the nurse beginning her care. In addition, the muffled conversation of the doctor's rounding was also evident at the bedside. Less than two minutes later an infant in C-Pod began crying. The nurse began her care by placing one hand under Josie's head and the other under her trunk and moving her up in bed. The sounds of rounds increased and the nurse proceeded in her care delivery by checking Josie's NG [feeding] tube.

As the nurse moved to remove swaddling and place the blood pressure cuff on Josie's leg, Josie began to hiccough. The extension and flexion movements of her arms and legs continued as she reached out momentarily to grab the monitor wire. The monitor of the child in the next bed began ringing and sounded intermittently over the next several minutes. Josie maintained her oximeter readings in the high 90s and the nurse increased the oxygen level in preparation for suctioning Josie's ET tube. Throughout the suctioning, Josie's oximeter reading was near 100, she made a slight grimace with her face and extended her leg, foot, and toes. After a second pass of the suction catheter, the nurse replaced the ventilator tubing and covered Josie's head and the upper portion of her face softly with a cloth diaper.

5. Behavior following caregiving: Within a few minutes of the completion of the care sequence, rounds also were completed, Josie's nurse left the bedside, and the movement near Josie's bedside ceased. Josie continued to be pink and appeared to be in a drowsy but restless state as she continued to hiccough over the next 5 minutes. As her hiccoughs stopped, so did Josie's extraneous movements. Her heart rate remained in the 160 to 172 range and her respiratory efforts were comparably steady, within the 37 to 62 range.

Summary: Josie is now 6 weeks old and 30 weeks post conception. Despite the fact that she continues to work hard to regulate her own respiratory efforts, Josie is also experimenting with interacting with her immediate environment visually and tactilely, by opening her eyes, beginning to focus, and grasping various objects within her reach. Josie's behavioral cues are clear and to her repertoire of signals she has added some wonderful facial expression. While noise and movement within the pod continue to result in changes in her behavior, Josie can use her self-calming strategies, bracing her feet, grasping, and sucking to regulate her state with some success.

Josie's parents continue to visit their daughter with great regularity. They recognize her behavioral cues and respond appropriately. They are also careful observers of Josie's development and are able to share pertinent observations that document her developmental milestones.

In a conversation to follow up on her report, the developmental specialist told us she felt Josie had "a real personality." Josie was doing a good job developing "coping strategies," the specialist told us, bringing her hands to her mouth, sucking on her ET tube, or extending her legs whenever she was stressed. The overall picture presented by the specialist was of a little girl who was very responsive to her environment, very aware of what was going on around her. She still belonged inside her mother, but she was doing her best to cope with the outside world she had been forced to enter too early. These are things we thought we already knew, of course, but it was reassuring to hear them confirmed by an expert.

At the same time that Kim and I were becoming more concerned about Josie's development and the quality of her day-to-day care, we also were getting a sense that we should be at the hospital more often, both to monitor Josie's progress more closely and to start playing a larger role in her care. At the end of June, we still were visiting Charlottesville twice during the week for the afternoon, and then overnight on weekends. But we were starting to sense that Josie needed us to be there more often and that it was good for her to have us there.

As it turned out, relatives of mine in Richmond had friends with a house in Charlottesville that was going to be vacant for July and part of August. They told us they would be happy to let us use it. Although we hadn't been unhappy with the Ronald McDonald House, having our own place sounded much more settled, much more comfortable. It was convenient to the hospital—just a five-minute drive away—and we felt we could come and go more freely.

As July got under way, we started visiting Charlottesville for two or three nights at a time over the weekends, while still visiting a couple of times during the week. Kim was making the three-and-a-half-hour round trip on her own some weekdays while I stayed home or went into D.C. and worked. It was getting harder for both of us not to be there as much as we could, especially now that the nurses were encouraging us to participate more actively in Josie's care by taking her temperature, changing her diapers, and even bathing her.

It was bathing Josie more than anything else that made us start to feel connected to our daughter. On June 29, Josie's one-month birthday, we bathed her for the first time ourselves. Instead of washcloths or a sponge, we used Q-tips and 2-by-2-inch gauze pads that we wet with water. With Josie still lying on her warming bed and still connected to the ventilator, the cardiorespiratory monitor, and everything else, we dabbed softly with the pads and swabs at our 2-pound girl, exploring every contour and crevice of her little body for the first time. I remember thinking it was like cleaning a precious painting or fresco, meticulously covering every inch but never wanting to rub too hard, never wanting to disturb.

When we had finished cleaning Josie's front, the nurse turned her over for us so we could do her back. Because this involved unhooking the ventilator and reattaching it once Josie's head was in its new position, the procedure caused her oxygen saturations to drop and her oximeter alarm to sound.

She recovered quickly once she was settled into her new position, and we were able to resume.

From time to time, I'd look up and notice that all the nurses were watching us. One of them told us later that what we were doing looked more like an all-over body massage than a bath. Whatever it was, Josie clearly enjoyed the experience as much as we did. She stayed calm throughout, and her oxygen saturations hovered at or near 100 the entire time; it was rare to see them stay so high for so long.

The bath was our first true indication that our baby was responsive to our touch in a positive way. Too often, the nurses said, NICU babies are agitated by any kind of touch, any kind of stimulation. They have been poked and prodded so much by so many people that they associate all human contact with bad things. This is why touching and holding them early—as early as possible—is so important.

The second time we bathed Josie, just a few days later, didn't go nearly as well. The nurses had just put a new ET tube down her throat, and the procedure had wiped her out. It was clear from the start of the bath that she didn't want to be bothered. One touch, no matter how gentle, and Josie's oximeter alarm would sound. It wasn't a big deal; we could do another bath another time. But it was the kind of thing that made you feel bad in a way, like you were causing problems for your daughter just by being there. And it reminded us that for every good day in the NICU, a day like Josie's first bath, there was a not-so-good day soon to follow.

Indeed, there were days in July when Kim and I could hardly bear to spend even a few minutes at our daughter's bedside. These were days when Josie was particularly aggravated by touch and noise, when voices around the bed or even the approach of the lab worker to draw blood would set her off. Her legs would kick and her little arms would flail, and you could see her sucking furiously on her ET tube to try to pacify herself. But it was no use. The monitor alarms would beep-beep-beep interminably, and often the nurse and respiratory therapist would have to intervene and bag oxygen into Josie's lungs just to bring her vitals back to normal. The best thing on these days was to sit dead quiet at the bedside or just to leave.

Was Josie in pain? Was she suffering? I asked this question of the nurses several times, and they told me they only had our daughter's visual cues and the monitor readings to go by. While she was on the ventilator, Josie couldn't cry like full-term babies to tell the nurses there was a problem or that she was experiencing pain or discomfort. They said they had to trust Josie to tell them something was wrong in the only language her body knew: the language of physical movements, skin color, and key vital signs such as her breathing and heart rates. She had to rely on her body and not her mind or her voice to communicate and to signal distress.

Fortunately, this was never a real problem for Josie. She was actually quite adept at communicating her displeasure with every tool she had. The nurses all joked that she was going to be a demanding one when she grew up. The fact that she responded to the least bit of noise and the least bit of stimulation suggested she was very aware of herself and her surroundings, very communicative if there was anything bothering her, and very intent on getting her rest, on growing. The nurses reminded us again and again that although it was no fun to see our daughter so obviously distressed from time to time, it was a lot better than the alternative, which would be to have Josie suffer in silence and alone, enduring every insult, every threat, and every painful moment without sending so much as a signal to the world outside.

It was July 6 when Kim got to hold our daughter for the first time; Josie was thirty-eight days old. Once before, toward the end of June, the nurse had allowed Kim to lift Josie in her hands and hold her in the air just inches above the bed. But we had never been able to remove her from the bed and hold her close against our bodies, *really hold her* like a baby should be held.

In the NICU, it's called "kangaroo care" or "skin-to-skin." The idea is to hold the baby's bare skin against your own so that your body temperature keeps her warm. Kangaroo care originated in South America at a time when incubators were in short supply. It's an idea that has slowly taken hold in the United States as more and more doctors and nurses see what it does for babies and parents alike—a low-tech intervention that gets parents actively involved in providing a positive experience for the child. Not only does it reinforce the bond between parent and child, it supposedly harkens back to the comfort of the in utero experience as the child hears the parent's heartbeat and feels the breathing and the warmth of another body.

"Doing the 'roo" with a child who is still intubated and on several IVs is a challenge. In fact, we found that some nurses—and doctors, too—still are uncomfortable with the idea; they think it is too stressful for the child. There are other risks as well, for example, an IV or an ET tube getting jiggled out of place or the fact that it's harder to get to Josie quickly if there's a problem.

Others, however, believe it's never too early to start parents and premature children on a healthy regimen of skin-to-skin contact. Although there were times when I wondered if the nurses were too quick to let us hold our baby, times when Josie might have been better off left alone, I can't help but think that holding her early helped Josie in a major way. It showed her that human contact is basically a good thing, not something to be afraid of; it showed her that other people weren't out to hurt her; and it introduced her in an intimate way to Kim and me.

The first few times we did it, we had two nurses and a respiratory therapist working with us. Just holding our baby became a major production. We set up a screen to shield us from the rest of the NICU. We checked to make sure all of Josie's IV and monitor lines could reach the chair where Kim would be sitting. If the IV lines wouldn't make it, we removed the IV pumps from their stands around the bed and placed them closer, sometimes on the bed itself.

Once we were certain everything was in place, the respiratory therapist disconnected the ventilator tubing at Josie's mouth and connected an oxygen bag in its place so he could keep pumping air into Josie while the nurses moved her to Kim. One of the nurses then lifted Josie up off the bed and placed her gently on Kim's bare chest, while the other nurse and I made sure all the tubes and monitor wires weren't getting tangled or caught. Once Josie was situated on Kim, the respiratory therapist reconnected the ventilator and we covered Josie's backside with a blanket to keep her warm. Everyone then took a fast look at the monitors to see how Josie had tolerated the move.

Kim's first skin-to-skin session with Josie was enormously successful. Josie seemed to love it; she was very mellow and sleeping with her cheek and hands on Kim's bare skin. The nurses were overjoyed to see Josie finally out of her bed and in her mother's arms where she belonged. Several of them peeked over the screen to get a look. One of our nurses told us later that it was one of the true rewards of her job to be on hand for life-changing moments such as a parent's first time holding a child or the first time a baby latches onto her mother's breast.

Nursing Progress Note. July 6: Parent bonding/skin-to-skin. Today Josie's nurse and physician discussed the benefits and appropriateness of Josie being held by Mom. At 1215, Josie was placed in skin-to-skin contact with Mom. She remained stable, against Mom's chest. . . . The trial continued for one and one half hours. . . . Her oxygen requirement did not increase, the number of desats that occurred were fewer than before being held. The patient tolerated being held without evidence of any problem. Mom and Dad enjoyed the experience tremendously.

A couple of days later, it was my turn to hold Josie. This time, she took a little longer to settle into the experience; her oxygen saturations and her heart rate dropped like a rock two or three times after the nurses placed her on me. At one point the respiratory therapist had to disconnect the ventilator and bag Josie with oxygen to bring her heart rate back up—all while she was lying on my bare chest. We later joked that Josie's initial discomfort was due to the fact that I didn't have breasts; I told the nurses my chest was about as flat as Josie's warming bed.

Once Josie and I both were settled, however, it was an enormously positive, once-in-a-lifetime experience. For two and a half hours, I sat quietly in a rocking chair in the middle of the NICU with my daughter sleeping on my chest. When they came to take her off of me, she grabbed hold of a couple of my chest hairs with her tiny fist and yanked them out like she didn't want to leave. They were still in her hand after the nurses settled Josie back into her bed—a souvenir of an experience that Josie and her father both had treasured.

Thursday, July 10: I feel we are at a high point right now, and I don't want to think too much about what that means. Yesterday, a group of medical students came through the NICU and one of the nurses was telling them about what happens there. She told them Josie was born very small and that she was doing quite well "at the moment." Her "at the moment" stuck with me. Later, the same nurse told us it is "very unlikely" that Josie will make it all the way through her stay at the NICU without an infection or another setback. It's something we knew already, but holding her this week and seeing her response makes you think everything will be fine. She may still be on the ventilator and all that, but you've got to think everything will be fine. You've got to believe she'll be all right.

Eighteen

Early in June, a story broke in the national media about a New Jersey teenager who gave birth in a bathroom stall in the middle of her prom, killed her baby, threw it in the trash, and then returned to the dance floor and ate a salad. The girl had somehow kept her pregnancy a secret from her family and friends.

I remember wondering at length how this girl could have considered her baby so expendable, a mere inconvenience. And I remember thinking about the enormous difference between what happened to that baby and what was happening to Josie. In Josie's case, no expense was being spared to save a child who would otherwise be dead. Meanwhile, in that New Jersey bathroom, a child who would have lived was killed and discarded without much thought at all.

If the experience of losing Nina and then watching Josie fight every day for her life taught me anything, it is that children are a miracle—not in a religious sense, necessarily, but in the sense that pregnancy and childbirth are wondrous works of nature. All too often, we lose sight of how we got here. The mere fact that human science has yet to replicate the nurturing environment of the womb is a reminder of just how special a process this is. Considering all the things that could easily go wrong, and that often do, every child that comes into the world on schedule and according to plan is a gift.

In a sense, the abrupt and tragic end of our pregnancy confirmed my earlier reservations about having a child. Before, I had considered it presumptuous and self-centered to think I could bring another person into this uncertain world to wing it along with everyone else. And now, months later, I had brought two people into the world, one to die after a forty-nine-hour struggle for life and the other to go on fighting and facing new insults and annoyances every day, more than most adults will ever see—all because Kim and I decided we wanted kids.

Thursday, July 17: Kim and I see these babies coming into the NICU with all sorts of problems and we start to wonder if anyone has healthy babies anymore. We are so deep into this now that it's hard to imagine there's another way. It's hard to imagine babies are born and aren't whisked immediately into the NICU, but instead go straight home. People don't know how good they have it when they take their babies home just a day or two after they're born. They don't even know this place exists where babies and parents are held together in limbo, where you're never 100 percent sure you'll ever take your baby home, and where every day is a reminder of the uncertainty of life.

As we settled into our routine of visits to Charlottesville, we started to become acquainted with some of the other parents in our area of the NICU. C-Pod had just eight beds in it for extremely low-birth-weight babies, so it was hard not to get to know the other parents and how they got there. From the start, it was apparent we all got there by different routes.

Next to Josie's station was a little girl, Laurie, who was born at home at a gestational age of between twenty-six and twenty-eight weeks. Her mother had been cramping for several days and went into the bathroom one morning and felt something hard. She called out to her boyfriend, who had to go find a flashlight so they could see better. And, sure enough, the "something hard" was the baby's head.

Laurie emerged in minutes right into her mother's hands. Her mother said she had a hard time getting herself to look down between her legs, but when she did, she saw this tiny baby with one eye wide open and looking at her. Laurie was breathing. Within minutes, a sister-in-law who lived downstairs arrived with a suction bulb—fortunately, she was a nurse—and she suctioned the baby's nose and mouth. Emergency response was there in ten minutes and wheeled mother and baby out of the house—the cord still attached and the baby still breathing on her own.

Another of Josie's suitemates was born at twenty-eight weeks weighing just 15 ounces; she had been growth-restricted in the womb. Another was a surviving twin, just like

Josie, a boy whose sister had died shortly after birth. As we introduced ourselves and started to get to know the other C-Pod parents, it was hard to know how much to ask about the events that had brought them there. We didn't want to pry, but at the same time, we had an irresistible urge to find out what happened to them. We were desperate to find company in our situation, others who were going through the same stresses and the same uncertainty as we.

There was a parents' group at the NICU that gathered once a week for coffee, but Kim and I never went. We found it more helpful to get to know the other C-Pod parents, the other parents whose pregnancies had ended very early and whose babies were born very small. There was a special kind of fellowship in C-Pod that I don't think we could have found talking to NICU parents whose babies were bigger and born closer to term. As far as we were concerned, the other NICU parents were dealing with entirely different issues, an entirely different set of problems. Their babies were fighting an entirely different fight.

It turned out that one of the other C-Pod couples, the Sheehys, were acquaintances of an aunt and uncle of mine. We became very friendly with them over time, getting together for meals in the hospital cafeteria and sitting and talking in the waiting area outside the NICU when the doctors kicked us out for their morning rounds. Kim and Sally, the mother, shared stories and frustrations about expressing milk for weeks at a time. The father and I joked about our freezers at home, which were filling rapidly with little containers of breast milk that we wondered if we could pour over cereal or into our morning coffee.

Getting into the raw details of our babies' outlooks and plans of care was still somewhat off-limits. Nevertheless, because the Sheehys had been in the NICU about six weeks longer than we, they could tell us more about some of the big milestones they had passed that were still ahead of us—everything from getting their daughter off the ventilator to getting her started breastfeeding. Although our babies were dealing with different problems and different prognoses, getting to know the Sheehys and their routine was like having a vision of ourselves just a few weeks ahead. When we were first getting to know them in June, Sally was at the hospital six days a week and was a very active participant in Ellie's care. She and Paul were starting to hold their little girl in a chair by her bed with few, if any, wires attached. It was a situation we hoped we'd be in soon.

We also became close with the mother of one of Josie's other suitemates, Ricky. He was the surviving twin. Ricky apparently had come into the world with so many checks against him that it was amazing he was still alive. He was born with a yeast infection and, as a result, had a major blood clot in his heart. They were pumping him full of blood thinners to get rid of it, but all that did was move part of the clot somewhere else, so now there were two. Ricky also had an enlarged liver and spleen because of all the drugs they had been giving him. And his mother told us he'd have to have eye surgery at some point because he had been on the ventilator for so long.

Ricky also needed surgery to fix the clot in his heart, but they wouldn't be able to do it until he weighed 8 pounds. He weighed just 4 pounds in June, so he and his parents had a long hospital stay in front of them. To make matters even worse, in May Ricky got pneumonia, an infection from the hospital, and they were just getting him over that.

Despite all this, Ricky's parents, Catherine and Rick, were

upbeat, open, and friendly. One Saturday night as they were leaving, the father stopped by our station and suggested we borrow some of Ricky's books to read to Josie. "Tell you a secret," he whispered to me. "Just read out loud and put your hand on their butt, and they're happy as can be."

Another Saturday night, we met Catherine's father. He was there with his daughter because Rick had to work that weekend. He and I stood off to the side while Kim and Catherine talked over Josie's bed, and he told me the family was worried about Catherine being in Charlottesville so much; they all lived in a small town that was more than a seventy-minute drive away. He told me she had been there every day but four since Ricky was born; Ricky was nearly two months old at the time. No one knew for sure if Ricky would be all right, he said. And he wondered, along with the rest of the family, if Catherine was becoming too involved. "I can't even imagine how she'd feel if something happened," he said.

Toward the end of June, there was a chicken pox scare in the NICU. A sibling of one of the babies became infected shortly after coming to visit. As a result, they had to clear out the entire NICU, section by section, to sterilize and clean it. When they returned our group to C-Pod after a few days in another section of the NICU, they moved Ricky to the station next to Josie's. He had been a couple of beds away and around the corner before. Now he was in Nina's old bed.

Apparently, Ricky's mother had told one of the nurses that she didn't want him there. She had seen Nina die and before that another child, both in the same spot. But it was the only spot where they could fit Ricky's special ventilator, so he had to go there. Ricky died two days later.

Tuesday, July 1: Ricky died last night. We knew he was having trouble, but we didn't expect the absolute worst. Kim was pretty shaken up when she heard; the fact that he was a surviving twin makes it that much worse. I came down late today from home in another car so I wasn't here yet. Poor Catherine. When we got to the NICU, Ricky's little station and bed were all cleaned up and cleaned out, just like they did with Nina. Like no one was there. This will take some time, I suspect, for Kim to get over. We were just getting to know Catherine and looking forward to seeing more of her and Rick, and now they're out of our lives.

Ricky's funeral was the following week. Kim felt that she wanted to go, but we decided against it and wrote Catherine and Rick a long note. Later, we heard through the nurses that Catherine said she wouldn't have traded anything for the eight weeks she spent in the hospital with her son.

The more time we spent in the NICU, the more I came to see it as a battlefield. These babies were soldiers fighting for their lives, valiant little warriors we were sending forth to live or die. Some of them would make it and some of them would not. Some would have battle scars that would be with them for life, while others would escape largely unscathed.

Thursday, July 10: Baby Rogers died this week. Kim was in the NICU that day and decided to leave for a while when there were ten or more people gathered behind the screen around the baby's little bed. She was the fourth baby to die, including Nina, since we've been in the NICU. I have enormous empathy for the parents, and I feel very fortunate that we are doing as well as we are, and that we had a second chance because of the twins. Having one baby and losing it, I imagine, would be enormously hard. Going home to the silence, to the toys and the baby books you won't need now.

One weekend, I watched out of the corner of my eye as Laurie's mother cried softly at her daughter's bedside. That morning, I had overheard the nurses saying Laurie had a major kidney problem and was going into surgery. It didn't sound good. I looked on from Josie's station as Laurie's mother stood to leave. Still crying, she bent over to give her daughter a kiss on the head. It was obvious from the way she lingered, not wanting to pull herself away, that she felt this was their final good-bye.

But Laurie survived. Just days later, the mother and father were gathered with friends around her bed and were laughing and talking about bringing Laurie home. Laurie was off the ventilator and was even crying from time to time that day. With all the other babies in C-Pod still on ventilators and silent, the sound of Laurie's wails was jarring and strange. All of a sudden, it was as if she didn't belong there. She was too well.

Monday, June 30: At the same time that there is bitterness and anger, there is an astonishment at people's good humor. Laurie's parents, after a tough week of near-death surgery for their little girl, today are laughing at her bedside. The other couples and the nurses are all giggles and smiles, sharing in Laurie's family's relief. You realize how resilient people are, how hard we all try to stay positive. And you start to see there are happy endings here.

Just as we were becoming friendly with some of the other parents, we also were starting to notice that there were babies in the NICU whose parents we rarely saw. By the end of June, we were in Charlottesville all weekend and for two or three days during the week. And we still hadn't seen some of the other parents. At first, I was inclined to give them the benefit of the doubt. Charlottesville, after all, is a regional medical center, and I knew for a fact that one of the other sets of parents lived more than three hours away. I could understand how work and other commitments, including other children, could keep parents from being there as much as they liked. But some of the parents, it seemed, didn't even try.

I remember thinking back to how Kim and I felt at first—how we weren't sure how much of ourselves to invest in Josie's progress, how we didn't want to be let down yet again. I remember thinking about those early visits to the NICU, both me alone and then with Kim, and how it was this strange and foreign place where I couldn't imagine spending lots of time. And I wondered if maybe these other parents never got over those early feelings, if they never really jumped in after dipping their toes and feeling the cold. I wondered if maybe they had no interest whatsoever in the place, if it was just a high-tech babysitting operation to them. They could call and check in from time to time, but visiting more than once every week or two would be too much. I imagined them justifying this by saying the baby shouldn't be born yet anyway.

"Why get all involved," I imagined them thinking. "We'll have our baby home soon enough."

Nineteen

On July 11, two days after I held Josie for the first time, they gave her an initial shot of steroids intended to help wean her from the ventilator. The steroids, which temporarily improve the functioning of the lungs, are given in a two-week cycle that provides a window of opportunity to get the baby breathing on her own when the doctors decide it's time.

By the morning of July 12, it was clear the steroids were

doing their job; Josie was requiring less and less ventilator support. The people from the lab were at her bedside every two hours to prick her foot for a blood gas. Every time the results showed that Josie was responding well to the latest round of downward adjustments in her ventilator settings—by maintaining a high level of oxygen in her blood and a low level of carbon dioxide—they would wean her even more.

Josie's nurse that day called the process of continually adjusting Josie's vent settings downward a "power wean." It was invigorating to watch at Josie's bedside as our daughter bravely presented the doctors and nurses with every indication she could that she was ready to breathe on her own.

Josie was taken off the ventilator for the first time since her birth on the evening of July 12; she hadn't breathed completely on her own for the first six weeks and two days of her life. Unfortunately, Kim and I weren't able to be in Charlottesville for the big event; we had friends from New England coming to stay with us for the night and had left her bedside around three o'clock that afternoon.

Josie's nurse reported in a five o'clock phone call that our girl was doing fine. "On tummy and resting comfortably," Kim wrote in Josie's book that evening after the call.

The move off the ventilator didn't mean Josie required no respiratory support at all. Instead of the ventilator and its mechanized breaths, Josie now had plugs in her nostrils to provide a constant flow of pressure to her lungs. Called C-PAP (for continuous positive airway pressure), the device is designed to keep the small air sacs of the lungs from collapsing after each breath. Developed by a UVA neonatologist, C-PAP essentially keeps the lungs inflated so the baby doesn't have to work so hard to open and close them. All Josie had to do now was breathe. And it seemed she was doing this without much of a problem.

At ten o'clock that evening, however, just as we were finishing a long and leisurely dinner with our friends, we received a call from Josie's night nurse. She told us Josie was having a lot of apnea and bradycardia episodes—as many as four every half hour—and that they might have to put her back on the ventilator. Josie had A-and-B spells through the night, the bulk of them requiring the nurse to intervene, either by bagging her with oxygen or by rubbing her shoulders, her back, or her feet to stimulate her central nervous system. By morning, it was clear that Josie's first time off the ventilator was a bust. Our daughter was reintubated at 6:45 A.M. on Sunday, July 13.

For weeks, everyone had told us that getting your baby off the ventilator is never easy. They had told us it often takes two or three tries before the baby can show she's ready. But there is something about being in a situation like ours that makes you think your child is different. You think your child will defy the odds. We had seen how well and how fast she responded to the steroids, and we, like the doctors and nurses, had become convinced that she was ready to put her ventilated days behind her.

Not only that, but we were eager for some good news. After everything else that had happened, we felt we were due. We felt we deserved for Josie to leap this next, all-important hurdle without a problem. We wanted her off the ventilator so bad that we were almost ready to pull the tube out of her throat ourselves. We felt she had already been on the machine long enough—too long, we feared—and we desperately wanted to see her breathing on her own.

We returned to Charlottesville the morning of July 13 to

be with Josie after her valiant try off the ventilator the night before. Kim held her quietly for two hours that afternoon. The plan now, the nurses told us, was to try to extubate Josie again on Tuesday—two days away. The doctors apparently wanted to keep trying while Josie was still on her two-week cycle of steroids. They had to act now, they felt, while the steroids were boosting Josie's lung function and breathing, and therefore increasing the chances that she'd be able to breathe on her own. Despite the stress of the night before, Josie's vent settings already were back in the low range when we arrived at her bedside Sunday afternoon. She seemed to be doing fine.

To increase Josie's chance of success off the ventilator, the doctors increased her dosage of aminophylline, the central nervous system stimulant that can prevent apnea and brady-cardia and make a baby's breathing more regular. On Sunday, one of the nurses told us that Josie's aminophylline level actu-ally had been in the low range when she was extubated the day before. In a fairly common instance of the NICU nurses second guessing the doctors' moves, she said it was probably a bad call to proceed without giving her more, considering Josie's history of As and Bs.

This is about when we started to get the idea that the practice of medicine in the NICU—indeed, throughout the hospital—is more art than science. When you start talking about your baby being in intensive care, everyone inevitably asks about all the technology and about all the amazing things doctors can do. But the truth is I was more amazed at what the doctors couldn't do, at what they didn't know about how our little girl would respond to various treatments and inter-ventions. You read about newborn intensive care and you get the idea we have mastered it, but that is so far from the truth it's laughable. This is improvisation, the doctors and nurses responding to various issues and problems with the tools they have, uncertain if they'll work. It's the babies, not the doctors or the technology, that are running the show.

Kim and I spent Sunday night at the house in Charlottesville and were planning to spend Monday night as well. We wanted to be with Josie when they took her off the ventilator on Tuesday. We felt a little guilty, I think, about Saturday night, about being home with friends instead of with her. She had gone through one of the roughest nights of her hospital stay with a strange nurse and with us 100 miles away. We wanted to be there Tuesday. We knew there wasn't a lot we could do, but we wanted to be at her side. And we wanted to see her breathe.

We arrived at the hospital Monday morning just to check in and, to our surprise, Josie was already off the ventilator. Her nurse explained that they had weaned her so low on the ventilator settings overnight that there was no place else to go; the only next step was to extubate. Josie was in the C-PAP, the plastic prongs held up her nose with an apparatus attached to small, round, Velcro patches that were glued to the sides of her face. The nurse told us that Josie had been very fidgety and agitated at first, continually trying to wiggle the C-PAP off her face, but now she was calm. Seeing the C-PAP for the first time—the way it held fast to her face and pushed hard against her nose—I realized we would shortly come to hate it as much as we did the ventilator. We could only hope this was a very temporary thing.

By Tuesday, they were trying a different C-PAP apparatus on Josie; she seemed always to be wiggling out of the other one, pulling it out of her nostrils. The new C-PAP had even longer prongs, but they were softer, and they didn't seem to bother Josie as much. Nevertheless, when I tried to hold Josie skin-to-skin on Tuesday afternoon, she was so uncomfortable we almost gave up. The nurse had taken off the C-PAP so she could move Josie from her bed to me. But, when we tried to get the prongs back up her nose while she was lying on my chest, Josie was furious. It was the first time I heard our baby cry. She was on my bare chest, wriggling around and screaming bloody murder. The nurse finally gave up and let Josie lie on me without the C-PAP, breathing perfectly well on her own. I guess she showed us.

Tuesday, July 15: You start to get a sense of a real personality there, a real spirit. Defiance. This girl isn't going to sit and take it. How else could she survive this horrific experience?

Over the next few days, the doctors ordered that Josie be given breaks from the C-PAP; they called them "room air trials." The idea was to see how she did breathing entirely on her own. They started by giving her one hour off the C-PAP for every eight hours she was on it, then an hour off for every four hours on, and finally two hours on, two hours off. Josie was doing fine—a few As and Bs, but no more than before. Better yet, Kim and I got to hold her during some of the trials. We hadn't yet held her without any ventilator equipment attached. It was so easy, so much more natural, and all that obscured her face now was the feeding tube through her nose and the tape that held it in place above her mouth.

On July 17, in a move that signaled the end of the acute-care phase of Josie's hospitalization, the doctors ordered that she be moved from her warming bed to an isolette, or incubator. She now weighed 1335 grams, or roughly 2 pounds 14 ounces.

Before becoming immersed in the ways of the NICU, I had assumed that incubators were reserved for babies in more critical shape, babies who need a more controlled environment, and who need to be more sheltered from their surroundings than their healthier peers. But the truth is that babies *graduate* to incubators from warming beds when the doctors decide that they no longer require constant attention. On a warming bed, which is essentially an open platform with a heat light above it, the baby is always easy to get to in an emergency situation, easy to manipulate. In an incubator, however, she's behind the plastic, and it can take precious seconds for a nurse to open the hatches or drop down the outside door to get her hands inside. And, once your hands are there, it's awkward, like working under a salad bar spit shield.

Between the escape from the ventilator and the move to Josie's isolette, Kim and I were feeling pretty good about things as we celebrated Josie's eight-week birthday on Thursday, July 17. Good enough to start talking to the nurses about the possibility of moving Josie to the hospital in Winchester, a little more than a half-hour drive from our home. Kim had toured the hospital's NICU earlier that week after a follow-up appointment with her doctor in Winchester and said she liked what she saw.

The possibility of moving Josie to Winchester had been mentioned early on. UVA's goal was to get her to a point where she was off the ventilator and stable, and it seemed we were finally there. Even though we still had the house in Charlottesville, Kim and I were getting tired of the distance between Josie and home. We were spending as many as four or five nights a week in Charlottesville. We were tired of eating all our meals in the hospital cafeteria and in Charlottesville restaurants. Our dogs, we imagined, were losing track of who we were; they were boarded at a neighbor's house up the road for eighteen of July's thirty-one days.

In Winchester, we could spend a lot more time with Josie, which everyone agreed would be good for all of us, and we could still be home and sleeping in our own bed. We imagined a new routine, with Kim going to the Winchester hospital during the day and then coming home for dinner so we both could visit our daughter at night. Meanwhile, I would be in my office on a more reliable basis and could catch up on work and do some writing.

I left on a weekend business trip to Phoenix on Friday, July 18 before we had a chance to talk to the doctor about a possible move. When Kim brought it up with him that afternoon, he said he didn't think it would be a problem. He said he wanted to wait about a week so they could get Josie up to full feedings; they were still supplementing her tube feedings with minimal amounts of the IV nutrients and lipids. Kim also talked to the NICU social worker about getting in touch with our insurance company to see if they would cover the costs of the move.

Kim called me that Sunday at 5:00 A.M. Phoenix time. I jumped up, startled, out of my hotel bed. She was at our house; she'd left Charlottesville early Saturday evening to go home and be with the dogs. I was due home late Sunday afternoon, and we were planning to head back to Charlottesville together Sunday night or Monday, depending on what was going on.

Kim said she had just spoken with Josie's night nurse and that Josie had had a horrible night. Kim was crying. "Another horrible Saturday night and we weren't there," she said, re-

membering Josie's first try off the ventilator just a week before. The problem, yet again, was a nonstop night of As and
Bs, although this week's episodes sounded more serious. The
nurses were intervening as much as every ten minutes to keep
Josie's vitals up, Kim said. She said this time they thought it
was an infection.

Kim was still crying. "Why can't we get one break?" she
said. "Just one break."

The nurses had started Josie on an all-purpose antibiotic,
vancomycin, as soon as the A-and-B episodes worsened. They
also had taken blood for a sepsis workup. The nurse told Kim
they'd know more in a day or so; that's how long it would
take to start seeing evidence of harmful bacteria in the lab
culture. Meanwhile, if Josie did have an infection, the antibiotics were already working against it. Josie's A-and-B spells had
already slowed a bit, the nurse said. She told Kim that was a
good sign.

Kim was unsure what to do, whether she should wait for
me or go to Charlottesville later in the morning just to be
there. We agreed she should go ahead and that I'd meet her
at the hospital; I'd drive straight there from the airport. Instead of going back to sleep, I got up and went for a run,
thinking it was only natural for this to happen the one time
all summer that I decided to go away.

I was at the hospital that afternoon by two o'clock and met
Kim in the NICU. Josie was doing much better. They had
taken her out of her isolette, removed her central line IV,
stopped her feedings, and put her back on the IV nutrients.
They also suspended the room-air trials off the C-PAP. Although all of these were backward steps, they all made perfect
sense. We just didn't want to see our baby back on the ventilator.

The nurses had the results of the sepsis workup by the time we visited Josie early Monday morning. The workup showed a *Staphylococcus aureus* infection, a fairly common type of acquired infection that shows up often in hospital patients. The vancomycin had apparently nipped it in the bud and Josie was doing OK. The nurses and doctors had acted fast on Saturday night at the first hint of a problem, and it paid off.

Monday, July 21: Josie is very clearly back to her fussy old self, fidgeting a bit and getting all hot and bothered by suction and the blood lady. It's hard to believe she had such a rough Saturday night; she would not have made it without the nurses having constantly to intervene. I know we were supposed to expect Josie would get an infection, but how could we have known it would be so hard on her?

On Tuesday morning, I stayed at the house in Charlottesville to do some work while Kim went to the hospital to check on Josie. The phone rang about an hour after she left. Before I could even say hello, Kim spoke up.

"You won't even believe this," she said, obviously stressed. "They're moving Josie into isolation."

Apparently, additional tests on Josie's blood had shown she had an MRSA, a type of staph infection that is resistant to certain antibiotics. Although Josie still seemed to be responding well to the vancomycin, the possibility of MRSA meant she had to be separated from the other babies, put in her own room with her own nurse.

Wondering when this all would end, I told Kim I'd be right there.

Josie's isolation room was a 12-foot square, just enough

space for her warming bed and a couple of chairs, along with all the standard bedside equipment. The room had its own scrub station and sink outside, and big windows so you could see out to the NICU and the nurses could see in. There was an intercom system and video camera, and all of Josie's monitors were wired to the main nurses' station outside so they could follow her vitals from there.

To be with our daughter while she was in isolation, we had to wash up, as usual, and then put on yellow, full-body scrubs, surgical masks, and latex gloves. We were able to touch and hold Josie, but not skin to skin. Kim immediately began to wonder about the impact this would have on the little girl. We were just getting in the habit of holding her as much as we could, and we were just beginning to understand how much she enjoyed it. Latex-to-skin just wasn't the same.

Also, the more time I spent in isolation—breathing in and out of the damn mask, sitting in the numbing silence of our private room, with people looking in from time to time, waving, like we were in a bubble—the more I felt woozy. I couldn't stand being there for more than twenty minutes at a time before getting up and going for a walk. We both hoped it would be over soon.

Josie, however, appeared to be doing just fine—no As and Bs, no desats, and happily sucking on a pacifier like any other healthy baby. By Tuesday evening, she was back on full feedings and two-hour room air trials. On Wednesday morning, after a night when Josie was giving the night nurse fits by trying constantly to wiggle out of the C-PAP—and succeeding more often than not—the doctors ordered that she be taken off it completely.

And so there we were, all gowned up, gloved, and masked as though Josie had some horrible disease, and our baby was doing better than ever. For the first time in her life, she was breathing entirely on her own.

Late Wednesday, they had the results from a Tuesday culture. It was negative; Josie no longer had the infection. Now they were doing additional lab work to find out for certain if it had been a resistant strain of bacteria. Apparently, many of the doctors and nurses were suspicious; one of the nurses told us she hadn't seen a true MRSA case in the NICU in more than five years. If it was confirmed as an MRSA, Josie would have to stay in isolation through the course of the antibiotics, or at least two weeks. On the other hand, if they could show it wasn't an MRSA, we'd be out of there as soon as possible.

We returned home Wednesday night and on Thursday morning got the call. The hospital's experts on infectious diseases had determined that it was indeed a false positive, Josie did not have an MRSA. The move to isolation had been for naught. The nurse who called Thursday told us Josie would be out of isolation later that morning and moving not to her old home in C-Pod with the other micropreemies, but to D-Pod, the last stop before home.

The weight cutoff for D-Pod is 1300 grams, or just shy of 3 pounds, and they like to see the D-Pod babies breathing on their own and feeding without any IV supplements. So Josie just made it. A week earlier, she would have missed on all three counts. To add to the good news, the nurse told us the doctors had given Josie an OK to start breastfeeding. We were floored.

Of course, we had no illusions we were going home any time soon. And we were sure the events of the week had delayed any move to Winchester. But it was an avalanche of good news to make up for the stress and strangeness of the week before.

Friday, July 25: C-Pod is full again. It may be a good thing we were pulled out of there when we were. They've had lots of new admissions, including a set of twenty-five-week twins just yesterday. Apparently, one of them didn't make it and the other is still fighting for life. It's a war zone, that place. I think we'll be glad we've moved on. With smaller and sicker babies coming in all the time, it's obvious Josie wouldn't get the same kind of attention she's had. It would also be more than a little unsettling, I think, watching another wave or two of new parents have to deal with issues that—we hope—are well behind us.

Twenty

Friday, July 25: We are in D-Pod now. It is quieter and darker—good things—but a little more crowded. There's less space around Josie's isolette to sit. Our nurses from C-Pod, Tricia and Andrea last night and then Rhonda this morning, keep stopping by to see how things are going. They say they miss little Josie. They say they miss us, too.

Last night it looked like Tricia was going to cry when she came to talk to us. We had all become so close. Then she left for two weeks and came back and Josie was in a whole new place, a whole new situation. It's hard to explain how much you bond with these nurses; for a time they are the most important people in your life. You're closer to them than family. And then they're gone. You're gone. And now the doctors are talking about getting us to Winchester as early as next week. It's all happening very fast.

Just when we thought our infection scare was over with the move out of isolation and into D-Pod, we received yet another reminder, as if we needed one, that you can't get too upbeat about your child's progress in the NICU. Bad news is always lurking around the bend. On Sunday, July 27, we learned that a routine workup on Josie's spinal fluid after the infection revealed something else that concerned the doctors; an entirely different bacterium was showing up in the culture. If the culture was right, Josie had meningitis. The doctors told us they'd have to do another lumbar puncture to know for sure.

Better known as a spinal tap, the lumbar puncture is among the more stressful procedures administered to babies in the NICU. It is customarily done as part of a sepsis workup to rule out infection or to make sure an infection hasn't crossed over from the blood to the spinal fluid and the lining of the brain. The procedure involves bending the baby over at the waist into a ball and then inserting a long needle into the lower back, between the bones of the spine, to withdraw spinal fluid. As often as not, the procedure is unsuccessful because it is so difficult to do. By the end of July, Josie had endured at least seven spinal taps; three or four of these were unsuccessful.

When we asked one of the interns about the worst-case scenario if Josie had meningitis, she told us it can lead to hearing loss, brain damage, and even death. She reassured us, however, that she didn't think this would be a problem for Josie, primarily because they had caught it early and she was still on a two-week course of antibiotics from the earlier infection. Besides, she was showing no outward signs of a continuing infection—no change in temperature, weird behaviors, or excessive spells of apnea and bradycardia. Everything looked normal.

By Monday, they had the results from a follow-up lumbar puncture, and the news was good. The white cell count in Josie's spinal fluid had decreased over the previous two days, meaning the infection was either gone or on its way out; there was nothing left for the white cells to ward off. Two of the doctors apparently disagreed about whether Josie had indeed had meningitis; one suspected the initial culture had been wrong. Nevertheless, they put us on another two-week course of antibiotics to stay on the safe side.

Kim put Josie to breast for the first time on July 25, when our daughter was nearly two months old. The idea was to start to get Josie acquainted with the *idea* of breastfeeding while we continued feeding her through the tube to her stomach. We weren't expecting she'd be able to latch on and get a meaningful amount of milk at breast for some time. But we wanted to get her started practicing as soon as we could.

The nurses told us it can take weeks for preterm infants to develop the skills and reflexes that make nipple feeding possible. Learning to suck, swallow, and breathe—in that order—is an enormous challenge for many of these kids. And it's something we all take for granted. It was funny how many times I tried to explain this to friends and family and then saw them working it out for themselves, their mouths and throats moving ever so slightly to simulate a suck, a swallow, and then a gasp for breath. It's an instinct we never think about, and yet one that can take an enormous amount of work and practice for a premature infant to acquire.

Our nurses told us that Josie's gestational age, thirty-two weeks at the end of July, was about the time that many premature infants are able to coordinate sucking, swallowing, and breathing. Bottle-feeding is even harder to master because the milk can flow into the baby's mouth more quickly; the baby has less control. As a result, most preterm infants can't begin to bottle-feed until they are at a gestational age of about thirty-four weeks. Even then, however, it's a good bet they're still getting much of their nourishment through a tube.

Breastfeeding and bottle-feeding take a lot out of a premature infant. Just as it takes time to learn the reflexes and the skills involved, it also takes time to develop the strength and the endurance to do it meal after meal after meal. And it's clearly better to have your baby gaining weight while she learns to nipple feed than to force the issue and wear her out.

Josie's initial attempts at breastfeeding, like most everything else in the NICU, were a group effort. Kim would sit in a large wooden rocker at Josie's bedside, and we'd pull up one of the rolling privacy screens. Either the nurse or I would then remove Josie from her isolette and place her in Kim's arms. As Kim put Josie to breast to see what she'd do, we'd use a small syringe to place drops of stored breast milk on Kim. Some of the drops dribbled over the nipple and into Josie's mouth. Others just sat there inviting Josie to lick, which she did from time to time. Even if she couldn't bring herself to suck long and hard enough to get milk from inside Kim, the drops on the nipple guaranteed that Josie was at least getting a taste, and we hoped she was starting to associate that taste with being at breast.

Once the get-acquainted session between Josie and Kim's breast had gone on for about ten minutes, we'd get ready to start the tube feeding while Kim kept Josie on her chest. The first order of business before we could "drop the feed" was to check the leftover amount, or aspirate, from the feeding before. To do this, the nurse would connect a 10-cc syringe to the end of Josie's feeding tube and pull up on the plunger to extract the contents of our daughter's stomach. This was still the one job I couldn't bring myself to do; I always imagined pulling up too hard and somehow extracting some of Josie's insides, too.

The amount of the feeding would depend on the amount of the aspirate. If all that came up through the syringe was air and bubbles, then we'd go ahead with a full feeding. At the end of July, Josie was supposed to be getting 28 cc, a little less than 1 ounce, every three hours. But if the nurse pulled on the plunger and the syringe started filling up with aspirate—normally just white and bubbly, mostly undigested milk—then we'd adjust the feeding amount accordingly. If there was little or no aspirate over a period of days, it meant the doctors could consider increasing Josie's feeding amount. It meant Josie was tolerating her feedings without a problem.

Next, we'd hook up the feeding tube to a larger, 30-cc syringe that we would either hold in the air or tape to the side of the rocker above Kim so that the milk would drain by the force of gravity into Josie's stomach. We'd then fill the syringe with warmed breast milk from the NICU refrigerator. By this time, Kim's shelf in the refrigerator was filled to capacity with little containers of expressed breast milk. Both of our freezers at home were, too. Each time we'd visit UVA, we'd come with a cooler-full of fresh stuff to replenish the NICU's supply.

A little push with the plunger at the start of the feeding, and the syringe would start draining slowly through the tube into Josie's stomach. Kim would still be holding Josie at her breast for the duration of the feeding, or at least until she got fussy. This to start creating a link in Josie's mind between a full belly and being at breast.

Friday, July 25: Tried breastfeeding today. It was a decent first effort, with Josie exploring and not getting too agitated about it. We can't expect miracles. Kim thinks if she does more pumping beforehand her nipple might be easier to latch onto. We'll try it again tonight.

At the outset, we were putting Josie to breast every second or third feeding while we were there and giving her a break for the feedings in between. There were some times when Josie would do practically nothing and others when she'd latch on for a few good sucks. This was the most we could expect at the time.

Each of the nurses had different ideas about how best to get Josie to latch on. Some would encourage Kim to hold Josie's head more firmly against her, giving her no choice but to get a mouthful of nipple. Others would get Josie started sucking on a pacifier and then try to transfer her to the breast. Still other nurses preferred the low-pressure approach, allowing Josie to explore while we dripped milk on Kim and dropped the feed. She'd get it soon enough, they assured us.

All the different ideas and all the different approaches to getting Josie to latch on didn't bother us at all—the more ideas the better—until a night in late July when one of the nurses was clearly out to prove she had the best technique. Kim and I had tried unsuccessfully for about ten minutes to get Josie interested, and we suggested to the nurse that we start the tube feeding. The nurse, however, insisted we keep trying. She then suggested that Josie might be having trouble because her feeding tube was in her mouth rather than her nose.

With Josie lying on her back on Kim's lap, the nurse pulled the oral feeding tube out and tried to insert a nasal one. Predictably, Josie's heart alarm sounded as the new tube went down; the nurse assured us this was merely a "reflex reaction." Josie then started turning blue around the eyes and I had to bring the "blow-by" oxygen apparatus up close to her face to bring her back.

Once the new tube was in, the nurse checked and found it wasn't in Josie's stomach; we'd have to do it again, she said. Kim and I were by then about fed up with what was happening, and we were aggravated that Josie hadn't yet gotten her food. Not only that, but I was concerned about the nurse conducting this invasive procedure while Josie was on Kim's lap. Several times, we had heard that it's important for these babies not to associate bad things with their parents. Let the nurses and doctors do the bad stuff so the only thing the parents mean to the kids is comfort and nourishment.

At our suggestion, the nurse did the new tube insertion with Josie in the isolette. This time it worked fine; listening to Josie's belly with her stethoscope while she pushed air through the feeding tube with a syringe, the nurse heard bubbles confirming that the tube was where it belonged: in Josie's stomach. She then encouraged us to try to get Josie to latch on one last time, giving her a pacifier and then transferring her in midsuck to Kim. It still didn't work so we went ahead with the tube feeding—about an hour after we had first taken Josie from the isolette. I imagined she was starving.

That night, I awoke around two o'clock and had trouble getting back to sleep. I was remembering Josie turning blue on Kim's lap and wondered if we had hurt her in some way or if she'd ever tolerate going to breast again.

Fortunately, when we were back in the NICU the following morning, everything seemed to be all right. At Kim's breast for another feeding, Josie was licking and trying to suck and resting her little hand on Kim's chest. My role, again, was to get her out of the isolette, drip milk on Kim's breast, and then set up the tube feeding. Kim was doing all the work, of course, but I felt I was getting quite handy at "nipple-dripping" and everything else. And I was happy I had a purpose.

Kim and I knew that the feeding was going to take time; we had to be patient. In the meantime, we were comforted that Josie was doing better than ever as we settled into D-Pod. She was sleeping soundly in her isolette and responding beautifully to being held. When we didn't put her to breast for a feeding, I would sometimes just hold her while we dropped the feed into her tube. Often, she'd sleep through the whole thing. It was a thrill to see her so relaxed, so calm.

Saturday, July 26: Today we gave Josie her first tub bath. She tolerated it beautifully. Josie is nearly two months old, and it was the first time we've seen her completely naked, without any IV's or monitor leads attached. She is an adorable little kid.

Being in D-Pod with a new set of nurses, we started to get a fresh sense of how lucky we were that Josie was doing so well. Without exception, the nurses spoke of Josie's progress as "unbelievable" and "amazing"; they were uniformly impressed that a twenty-four-weeker like our daughter had come so far with no readily apparent problems; she was out of danger and starting to feed.

One afternoon while I was holding Josie, I had a long conversation with one of the veteran D-Pod nurses about how things had changed since she started working at UVA thirteen years before. In her first years getting babies and their parents ready for home, she and the other D-Pod nurses never saw infants born before twenty-eight weeks gestation; they just didn't make it. Babies coming in at 3 or 4 pounds were considered very small. She said it would have been extremely rare even five years before to see a twenty-four- or twenty-five-weeker come through D-Pod. And to see them come through with few obvious problems was still a rarity, as far as she was concerned.

Saturday, August 2: The August interns started the other day, and Josie's nurse said it was sort of funny watching them get briefed about our daughter's history. Standing around her isolette with the attending physicians and the nurses recounting all the gory details about Josie's early weeks, the interns' jaws dropped and their eyes opened wide as they all leaned in for a closer look, unable to believe that the quiet, cherubic-looking child before them was the same one the doctors were talking about.

Although we were feeling fortunate about our daughter's remarkable progress during her first two months, there were still concerns. Josie's continuing struggle with apnea and bradycardia was a source of continuing stress and aggravation. We'd be feeding her or holding her or just standing quietly by her isolette, and out of the blue the monitor alarm would blare to tell us her heart rate had dropped by half or more. It usually turned back around within seconds, but there still were many times—once or twice a day—when the nurse or we would have to intervene and stimulate Josie in some way to bring her back.

Knowing that the hospital generally didn't discharge babies until they went eight days without an apnea or bradycardia episode, we wondered how Josie's inability to kick the condition would affect the schedule for getting her home someday. And we wondered how all the A-and-B episodes—no matter how quickly they resolved—might be affecting her, depriving her brain and other organs of the oxygen they needed to grow and develop right.

On July 25, the doctors ordered Josie off the IV of aminophylline, the central nervous system stimulant that is supposed to help prevent As and Bs, just to see how she'd do on her own. She'd been on the drug since early June. By July 28, they had her back on an oral version of the drug called theophylline; she was still having too many episodes. A downside of the theophylline is that it made her tachycardic, meaning it accelerated her heart rate. There were times when Kim and I would be holding her, and her heart rate would be humming along in the 200 range, clearly working overtime.

A new concern that emerged as we were settling into D-Pod had to do with Josie's eyes. We had been informed early on that many premature babies wind up with eye problems later in life, including nearsightedness, crossed eyes, loss of peripheral vision, or even blindness. The problem is something called retinopathy of prematurity, or ROP. In babies who have the disease, the normal development of blood vessels in the back of the eye is interrupted shortly after birth, and abnormal new vessels start to grow. If this continues, it can lead to bleeding and the formation of scar tissue that pulls on the retina. In the most severe cases, the retina becomes detached, causing blindness.

No one understands exactly why certain babies develop ROP, although it occurs most commonly in babies, like Josie, who receive supplemental oxygen and is believed to be closely associated with increased oxygen levels in the blood. It used to be that premature babies were given a constant flow of supplemental oxygen no matter their condition. They'd be placed in isolettes and fed 100 percent oxygen day and night. But then people started to notice that a lot of these babies were having eye trouble. This is why the nurses and doctors don't like it when a baby is on the ventilator and the reading on her oximeter hovers in the high 90s or at 100 for extended periods of time; they prefer it in the 88 to 95 range. To bring it down, they'll adjust the oxygen level on the baby's ventilator closer to room air.

Checking for ROP is like something out of a horror movie. The ophthalmologist places a metal clamp in the baby's eye to keep the lids open and then manipulates the eyeball with a paper clip or similar-sized tool while he shines a blinding beam of light into the eye to get a good look with his magnifying glass at what's happening back around the retina. All this while the baby screams bloody murder. The nurses normally encourage the parents to leave for the procedure. I generally stuck around, although I don't really know why. I could never bring myself to watch.

Wednesday, July 30: Some nights, I'll be lying in bed and thinking nonstop about the stress on little Josie. The past three days alone, there was that horrible eye test Friday, then the feeding tube episode on Kim's lap on Saturday, and another lumbar puncture Sunday morning. I just want to see her go through one day—just one day—when she is not manipulated or stressed in a big way. You have to wonder about the impact of all this developmentally, psychologically. It's the stuff of your worst nightmares.

After Josie's first eye exam on July 12, the ophthalmologist reported that her eyes looked to be in "good shape." He did notice a small amount of "damage," as he called it, in the left

eye and said he'd follow up two weeks later. Although one of
our nurses confided that blindness was a distinct possibility
for very early babies like Josie, another assured us that she
had rarely seen kids leave the NICU with serious eye problems.

Whatever the case, the nurses all agreed that it was a good
bet that Josie would wear eyeglasses, perhaps even as a tod-
dler. Kim and I both wear glasses, so this would not come as
a complete surprise. But we wouldn't know until later if Josie
would have more extensive eye problems. The plan was for
regular follow-ups as long as she was in the hospital, and most
likely even after she got home.

If potential problems with Josie's eyes weren't enough to
keep us up nights, we also were becoming increasingly concerned about her ears. Time and again, we'd been told that
infections and even antibiotics can affect these infants' hearing. We knew that Josie had responded to noise in the past,
regularly becoming agitated in C-Pod when there were loud
conversations and lots of activity around her bed. But after
the infection and all the antibiotics and once Josie was in her
quiet isolette, we weren't so sure any more.

One night in D-Pod, they were getting one of Josie's
neighbors ready for discharge, and they hooked the baby up
to a home apnea monitor to show the parents how it worked.
I was sitting and holding Josie at the time, and all of a sudden
the monitor alarm went off—a shrill, piercing noise intended
to wake parents from even the deepest sleeps to attend to their
child's breathing difficulties and, if necessary, to administer
CPR. Josie didn't so much as startle; she just kept on sleeping.

Knowing that they couldn't administer a hearing test until
Josie was bigger, any concerns we had about her ears had to

be temporarily put aside, along with other worries about the long-term developmental impacts of her troubled start in life.

Wednesday, July 30: Bringing home a blind, deaf, or severely disabled child is not something I can even think about right now. I just can't worry about these things until someone tells us we have a real problem. You tuck these worst-case scenarios way in the back of your mind and hope you never have to go there. You know they're there. You know they're a real possibility. But you keep the door closed. You've got enough to worry about as it is.

Our continuing concerns about Josie's development, her A-and-B episodes, and her progress learning to feed were in stark contrast to the concerns of many of the other parents in D-Pod. For these other couples, the place was just a quick pit stop on the way home for their babies, most of them born near term, but with relatively minor problems breathing, feeding, or fighting jaundice.

A couple we knew from our parenting class in Shenandoah County passed through the pod with their 9-pound baby boy for a couple of days. He had been born in the hospital back home, but was having enough trouble breathing that they sent him to Charlottesville for treatment. Three times the size of Josie, he looked like a monster to us. He was in and out of D-Pod and headed for home in a period of forty-eight hours.

Watching the other parents, we suddenly wanted out. We were at a point where all of Josie's "buddies," the three or four babies whom she'd been with in C-Pod from the start, were getting ready to leave. And we were starting to wonder if we'd be alone soon—just us and Josie and a constantly changing cast of relatively healthy babies, all of them just breezing through.

Friday, August 1: Little do these other parents know how good they have it. I look across the unit at the tiny, sick babies over in C-Pod—and even across the room we're in now at some of Josie's buddies who've been here as long or longer and now are getting ready for home—and I am reminded yet again how much we all take for granted. Nobody gets it until they have to stare it in the face, I mean really confront it themselves.

And I suspect that even they don't get it, these other parents who have been through the NICU with their babies for a couple days or even a week. All they are thinking is it's an inconvenience. There are no lessons here for them. I imagine them thinking they are different. Their babies are basically healthy. I imagine them thinking that these others, Josie and the rest, are dealing with problems they could never possibly encounter themselves. I imagine them thinking they did everything right. And I imagine them wondering about Kim and me and the other parents who've been here so long. I imagine them wondering if we did something wrong.

On July 31, we finally got the OK from the UVA doctors to move Josie to Winchester. They had been waiting for her apnea and bradycardia spells to subside a bit. They felt it would be a struggle to deal with them during the two-hour ambulance ride north, always having to intervene to stimulate her or give her oxygen. Earlier in the week while we were home for a day, Kim and I had visited with the Winchester neonatologist, Dr. Chilton, and her nurse practitioners. Kim had been there once before. Both of us came away impressed.

The night before we left Charlottesville, Josie's primary nurse, Tricia, got her all dressed up and paraded her through the NICU to say good-bye to everyone; apparently, this is a NICU ritual for departing patients. The next morning, Kim and I fed Josie one last time in D-Pod before placing her in her high-tech traveling isolette. The plan was for Josie to make the trip to Winchester with a nurse in UVA's special newborn ambulance; Kim and I would follow at our own pace and meet up with Josie once she was settled into the NICU there.

When Josie's "transport nurse" told us the traveling isolette had room for just one of her many toys, Kim and I selected a nest of baby birds, a finger puppet, that had been a fixture at Josie's bedside since early June. Everything else, the stuffed animals, outfits, and toys, we packed into two large "patient belongings" bags and piled them onto a rolling cart with a Styrofoam picnic cooler we'd loaded to the top with ice and full containers of Kim's breast milk. Kim's shelf in the NICU freezer was now empty.

Together with the transport nurse and another nurse who had been taking care of Josie that morning, we wheeled the isolette and the rolling cart through C-Pod on our way out of the NICU. The doctors and nurses were in the middle of their morning rounds—all gathered in a tight circle around one of the baby's beds and conferring about his condition and plan of care. They all stopped and looked up as we paraded through.

I remember a split second of suspended silence, like the moment at the very end of a virtuoso live performance when the crowd is getting ready to applaud. This was it. Josie Woodwell was moving on. They had taken care of her for nine weeks, seen her through a time when it wasn't at all clear she'd make it, and now she was a little over 3 pounds, a cute little kid, and moving closer to home.

I remember the smiles and everyone approaching Josie and us in a rush to say their good-byes. I imagined them thinking this was what it was all about, that despite the ever-present specter of death and disability and all sorts of untold horrors along the way, this was a place that gave life to these kids, that gave them a chance. These people had helped Josie surmount the toughest challenges she'd ever face. It was because of them that she had lived. And it was because of them that she was doing so well.

Several of the nurses leaned over Josie's isolette to say their high-pitched good-byes to our little girl. A couple of the others, nurses who had taken care of Josie time and time again and who had become trusted caregivers as well as friends, approached Kim and me with their arms outstretched. I closed my eyes to hold in the tears as I hugged them one after the other, but it was no use. I missed these people already. Not only had they saved my daughter's life, but they had taught me something about my own. They had taught me to care, to try to do something worthwhile and fulfilling with my days. And together with the doctors, they had shown me once and for all that life is precious—precious enough to be saved, no matter the cost.

Twenty-One

The Winchester NICU was a stunning contrast to UVA's. When Josie first moved in, she was one of just five babies in the entire unit; the UVA NICU, by comparison, generally cared for between forty and sixty babies at a time, albeit in several different walled-off areas.

The Winchester NICU, with just twelve beds in all, offered a much quieter, less intense environment than the environment we'd become accustomed to at UVA. The focus, as in UVA's D-Pod, was on "developmentally appropriate" care and getting families involved on a daily basis so they're ready to take their children home. Although the doctors and nurses regularly had to deal with all the standard problems and crises affecting premature and sick newborns, this wasn't a life-saving operation in the same sense as UVA's C-Pod. We later learned that Josie's size at birth, 1 pound 6 ounces, made her the lowest-birth-weight baby they had ever taken care of in the Winchester NICU.

Winchester is where Josie would have ended up from the start if she hadn't been born so early. The hospital generally doesn't accept babies born before twenty-eight weeks gestation because the facility can't offer surgical services for these infants. It sends them to UVA for that. Considering Josie's need for fast surgery after her bowel perforated when she was just a week old, it's clear she would have died if we'd had her in Winchester. They wouldn't have been able to save her.

The layout of the Winchester facility was disarmingly simple. There were no separate pods here, just one long, rectangular room with spaces for six babies along each of the side walls. The lighting was generally low and the floor and walls were gray, with a border of teddy-bear wallpaper running the length of the room. Established in 1995, the unit had an unmistakable feeling of newness to it. The isolettes, monitors, and the other equipment were of an entirely different vintage than those at UVA. Little PC screens above each baby's station provided a multicolor snapshot of all of her vitals at once. No longer did we have to deal with separate oximeter and cardiorespiratory monitors or abide the harsh wake-up call of the UVA alarms. The alarms on the equipment in Winchester sounded more like elevator chimes or doorbells, almost pleasing.

I remember thinking as we settled into Winchester with Josie that the UVA NICU had the aura of an old college dormitory, with lots of comings and goings, lots of clutter. It may have been hard to concentrate and even harder to relax, but there was always someone to talk to, always something going on. Winchester, by comparison, was like a well-appointed, off-campus apartment—very quiet, very neat, and with another level of amenities. But it was also sort of lonely in a way, at least in the beginning, before we got to know the nurses and some of the other parents.

We knew this was where Josie needed to be, but at the same time Kim and I missed our nurses and the friends we'd made at UVA. We missed the diversions, the rush of activity, and, most of all, the relationships that made our experiences in Charlottesville so much easier to bear. We doubted we'd be able to create the same rapport with the nurses and the other parents in Winchester.

From the start, however, our relationship with Josie's doctor in Winchester was a vast improvement over what we had become used to at UVA. In Charlottesville, we rarely interacted with the attending physicians, and we quickly learned that the young interns assigned to our daughter—there was a new one each month—knew no more, and often less, than Josie's nurses about her progress and her plan of care. When we had asked one of them about retinopathy of prematurity, she photocopied for us several pages from the NICU parenting book we already had. But in Winchester, it was clear that Dr. Chilton was running the show. We still interacted principally with Josie's nurses and the nurse practitioners, but

Dr. Chilton, it seemed, was always near and would talk to us most every day.

On Josie's first afternoon in the NICU, Dr. Chilton sat at a rolling table in the reception area for two hours going through the 4-inch stack of medical records UVA had sent along with our daughter. She then came over to Josie's bedside for a detailed discussion with Kim and me about her key goals for Josie. She said the number-one priority was to get Josie feeding and growing on her own. She also wanted to get Josie to the point where she could maintain her temperature so they could move her from the isolette to an open bassinet or crib. Another priority was to help Josie conquer her As and Bs once and for all.

We rapidly settled into a new routine once Josie was in Winchester, with Kim driving up during the day to work with her on breastfeeding and the two of us returning after dinner, either for more work breastfeeding or for some quality time holding or bathing our daughter. Everything revolved around Josie's feeding schedule. As of August 5, she was up to 31 cc, just over 1 ounce, of breast milk every three hours. And she was just starting to wake up on her own, often fussy and hungry, at around the time the next feeding was due.

The feeding regimen was pretty much the same as at UVA. Kim would work with Josie at breast for ten or fifteen minutes before we'd connect a new syringe to Josie's feeding tube and fill it with the prescribed amount of warmed breast milk. The nurse or I would then sit beside Kim holding the syringe in the air while Josie remained at breast and the milk drained slowly into her stomach. All of this was done behind a rolling screen.

It was generally before Josie's feedings, when she was

awake, when the nurses and we would change her diaper and check her temperature and the rest. If there were medications to administer, this was when the nurses would do it. Josie was now on a schedule of having her vital signs logged by the nurses every twelve hours. She was weighed and got a bath every twenty-four hours, at night.

The focus on breastfeeding at Winchester might have meant that I didn't get as much of a chance as before to hold and interact with Josie, but this wasn't the case. When Kim and I were there together, she'd often hand Josie to me before we'd start the tube feeding and after our daughter had had some practice at breast. I would hold Josie for the duration of the feeding and beyond, sometimes for as much as an hour or two, and sometimes skin to skin. There were even times when I was in the NICU alone. On the day or two each week that I had to be in D.C. for work, I'd stop in Winchester on my way home for Josie's nighttime feeding.

Wednesday, August 6: I held Josie skin to skin for more than an hour yesterday. We both enjoyed it enormously and I hope to do it again soon. I had the screen around me and was thinking it's odd how Kim and I aren't totally bothered to have these intimate moments with our child in a room with lots of other people and noise and lights. If you had asked me months ago whether Kim and I were fit for parenting in a public place like this, I'd have told you no way. But the fact is you adapt. You have to adapt or else you'd go nuts.

Tuesday, August 12: I had another "solo outing" with my little girl last night. It was great. I changed her diaper, got her out, and sat with her for more than an hour while she fed. She was very alert at first so the nurses took a picture to take home to

*mom; apparently, Kim had been complaining all day about how
sleepy Josie was. She laughed when I brought home the photo of
our wide-eyed little girl. The nurses wrote a caption on the photo:
"To Mom: I sleep all day and am awake nights."*

Like the nurses we had encountered after graduating to
D-Pod at UVA, the nurses in Winchester were uniformly
amazed that Josie was doing so well. Once they learned she
was born at twenty-four weeks and had experienced such a
troubled start, they'd tell us they couldn't believe she hadn't
had any brain bleeds or other problems. And I realized it was
very rare for these nurses to see a baby like Josie, a baby who
was so at risk. Every time they said it was remarkable how
Josie was doing, it reminded Kim and me of how lucky we
were—that despite the frustrations with feeding and the worries about the future and everything else, we had a real fighter
there, someone special.

As we settled into life in our new home away from home,
several of the nurses said they were impressed at how confi-
dently Kim and I handled Josie: changing her diaper and her
clothes, taking her temperature, getting her out of the isolette
for her feedings, and calmly stimulating her out of an apnea
or bradycardia spell. We told them our confidence was a tribute to the Charlottesville nurses and the way they encouraged
us to play a hands-on role in Josie's care from early on. It
was also a tribute, of course, to the fact that Josie had been
around so long. We'd had a lot of practice.

During the second week of August, the Winchester NICU
admitted a pair of twin boys; they were transferred from a
military hospital in the South where they hadn't been touched
or handled by their parents for two months. It's not that the

boys were in especially critical condition, it's just still that way at some hospitals. The doctors and nurses are so intent on allowing these babies to recover from their often-traumatic births and grow undisturbed that they forget what else these babies need. They forget about the importance of positive human contact and bonding between parents and child, or at least they decide these things aren't as important.

Starting shortly after the twins were admitted, we regularly overheard the nurses talking about how it showed that the boys hadn't been held, that they hadn't had much if any positive stimulation to counter all the negative and painful goings-on with which they were welcomed to the world. The boys were easily irritable; their cries and screams often filled the NICU.

The nurses said the boys had no "modulation" in their behavior; either they were asleep or they were awake and agitated. Despite patient confidentiality rules that discouraged hospital personnel from sharing information about other patients, the nurses and nurse practitioners often brought up the twins when they were talking to us about Josie's progress. They'd mention the twins' moods and their irritability, and they'd tell us it was a tribute to what had happened at UVA— all the holding and the focus on getting Kim and me involved—that Josie was doing so well.

From their first day in the NICU, the twin boys exerted a special pull on Kim and me. This is what we had lost when our pregnancy ended so soon, when Nina died. They may have been colicky and irritable and all the rest, but they were twins and would always be twins. From time to time, the nurses put them in the infant swing that made its way around the NICU. The boys would sit and swing together, their eyes closed and their heads resting one on the other. I'd remember the thought of Josie and Nina together inside Kim, always touching. And I'd wonder again how it would affect Josie, now alone in her isolette, that she'd lost her twin.

Twenty-Two

The Winchester NICU was our home away from home for longer than Kim or I imagined. By early September, Josie weighed 5 pounds and had been moved from her isolette to an open crib. Feeding was the major remaining hurdle she had to overcome before we could take her home, and she was still in practice mode into mid-September, never latching on at breast for more than a few seconds before she got tired.

Josie's A-and-B spells were another concern. She was still having a worrisome number well into September, perhaps five or six a day. Although most of these happened when Josie was feeding and was obviously stressed in some way, there were times when she'd be sleeping or lying quietly in my arms and her heart rate would go into a tailspin, causing the alarms to sound and the nurses to look up from what they were doing.

Last but not least, we also were becoming increasingly concerned about Josie's eyes. During her first eye exam in Winchester in late August, the doctor had found additional "damage" in Josie's left eye. In passing, he brought up the possibility of vision loss, glaucoma, crossed eyes, and other potentially nasty outcomes. After a follow-up appointment on September 9, he told us that the right eye was the same but that the left again was slightly worse. We weren't yet at the point where Josie would need laser surgery, but it was something he still wanted to watch very closely. He scheduled another follow-up in two weeks.

Tuesday, September 9: To go through all this and not to have Josie come out of it all right—with eyes, ears, and everything else working pretty much as designed—I fear would be an enormous blow. I don't even want to think about it. The eye doctor said it's important for Josie to keep growing, that her growth will help her eyes, and so now I'm supersensitive about Josie's weight gain. If she's not gaining consistently, which she really isn't right now, I worry how that might be affecting her vision. You can tell she's responding to light. You can tell she sees. You just can't tell how much she sees or how well. And now we have to wait another two weeks on pins and needles to find out more.

The lack of progress with breastfeeding and everything else made me increasingly worried about Kim. As of September 5, she had been in Winchester every day but one for the past month. She had Josie at breast for three or four feedings a day and was still having trouble getting her to latch on and suck for more than a few seconds. She was obviously frustrated. To reassure her, everyone kept telling Kim that a light would go in Josie's head one day and that she'd get it.

Then, around September 20—a week after Josie and her sister had been due—something remarkable happened. All of a sudden, Josie was latching on and eating with a vengeance. The light we had been told about for so long was now burning bright. Josie had finally decided it was time for her to move on.

On Wednesday, September 24, we got word from one of the nurses that Josie would probably be coming home the following week. The feeding had been going much better now for several days, and, at long last, Dr. Chilton and the nurses were happy with Josie's day-to-day weight gain; she now tipped the scale at about 6 pounds. Moreover, the doctor apparently hadn't seen any A-and-B spells that were of great concern over the previous week.

An additional boost came with the news that Josie's hearing was fine and that her eyes were improving. The eye doctor told us he was pretty sure Josie wouldn't need treatment. He said her condition was resolving itself, although he wanted us to schedule a follow-up appointment once Josie was home so he could be absolutely sure.

We could hardly believe it was all true. Josie would be coming home without any obvious checks against her, without any outward signs that she had just survived a grueling four months when it was never clear until the final days that she'd be all right.

The following Monday, Kim and I received training in how to use a home apnea monitor, and we were checked into a hospital room with our daughter for the night to make sure we were comfortable taking care of her. On Tuesday morning, after a sleepless night spent passing our baby back and forth between us just to hold her, we packed up Josie's things and left in the car for home—125 days after she and her sister were pulled into the world too soon.

Epilogue

Kim and I had an all-day party to celebrate Josie's first birthday in late May 1998. We set up a party tent out by the barn, hired a local bluegrass band, and served chicken barbecue to about a hundred family, friends, and neighbors. We considered the event a big thank-you to everyone who had been there for us and Josie and Nina during our four months in the hospital and while we settled in at home. And we saw it as a chance to show everyone how their help, their support, and their prayers had paid off for Josie.

The guest of honor had just started sitting up on her own. She wouldn't be walking or uttering any real words for another year. Despite the obvious delays, the doctors and the physical and speech therapists we saw regularly assured us that Josie was progressing all right, considering everything that had happened, and that as long as she kept progressing there was little for us to worry about.

Today, Josie is four years old. The only outward sign of her difficult start is the brace she wears on her lower left leg to help her walk. As it turns out, Josie has very mild cerebral palsy, meaning that at some point during her hospitalization there was some damage to the right side of her brain. This, in turn, has affected her control of her muscles on the left. Although the problem is not readily noticeable in her use of her arms and hands, Josie walks on her toes and with a slight limp when she is not wearing the brace. It is too early to tell how much of an issue this will be for her as she continues to grow.

Mild as it is, Josie's cerebral palsy hasn't proved much of a barrier to her healthy development and growth. She is a willful and playful little girl whose interests run the gamut from reading books and diapering her dolls to having you push her so high on her swing that you think she'll fly out of it and into the clouds. It's easy to forget sometimes how fortunate we are that Josie is doing so well.

Today, Kim and I have yet another reason to feel fortunate: Josie has a younger brother named Dean. Born in October 1999, Dean came into the world after a remarkably uneventful pregnancy during which Kim showed no signs whatsoever of developing preeclampsia or HELLP syndrome. Despite the two-and-a-half year difference between them, Dean is rapidly catching up to Josie in size. And Josie absolutely loves him to pieces.

In the years since Josie and her sister were born, Kim and I have had lots of time to reflect on everything that happened and to put Nina's death behind us as we focused intently on Josie's—and now Dean's—development and growth. One of the things I realized as time went on is that I had developed and grown some myself.

If you had asked me before all this happened, I probably

would have told you that our society was spending too much time and money saving babies who ought to be allowed to die. I probably would have suggested that modern medicine had gone too far—that simply having the technology and the know-how to keep these tiny beings alive wasn't justification enough.

Now, of course, I am not so sure. Having lost our Nina and having seen firsthand the many horrors that can—and often do—accompany an extremely premature birth, I fully understand and sympathize with those who say that these babies and their families might be better off in the long run if we simply allowed nature to take its course. Would Nina and we have been better served if the doctors and nurses had simply let her die instead of subjecting her to forty-nine hours of intensive treatment? Of course.

But hindsight's 20/20 and the fact that Josie is with us and is doing wonderfully shows why the doctors and nurses do this. Josie's medical care from the time she was born until the day she was released from the hospital in Winchester cost our insurance company more than $300,000. Kim and I paid less than 1 percent of that total, or about $3,000. Is this fair? Is it right for one child to run up such an enormous hospital bill while others struggle to get even the most basic forms of care?

Obviously, I am not qualified to answer these questions, believing as I do that Josie was worth every cent. But they are important questions just the same. And they are not the only questions that the events of the summer of 1997 have forced me to think about in a different way.

Just a few years ago, I wondered whether the good things in life outweighed the bad or whether life was special enough to justify bringing others into this world. Now I know that life itself is what justifies life. Josie and Dean have given me reason to live. I am eager to see what they become and how they make their own lives matter. And I am eager to help them in any way that I can.

As for Nina, all I can say is that shortly after we lost her, I came across the words of an unfinished song that the great Jimi Hendrix was working on the night before he died. Called "The Story of Life," the song closed with the following lines that immediately made me think of Nina—not only because of the words themselves, but because they never had the opportunity to be set to music, to truly live:

> *The story of life*
> *is quicker than the wink of an eye.*
> *The story of love*
> *is hello and goodbye.*
> *Until we meet again.*

Kim and I will never forget about Nina and the hopes and dreams we had for her. But right now our lives revolve almost entirely around Josie and Dean. And the challenge we live with every day is never to take their lives—or our own—for granted.